Animal Kingdom
Coloring Adventure

Introduzione

Welcome to "World Animals: A Coloring Journey"!

If you're here, it means you're ready to embark on a never-ending journey through the amazing animal kingdom.

We can't wait to share our discoveries and thoughts with you about the world of animals.

Thank you for choosing this book and for joining us on this journey.
We're sure you won't regret it!
Enthusiastically,

Simone Fiorentino

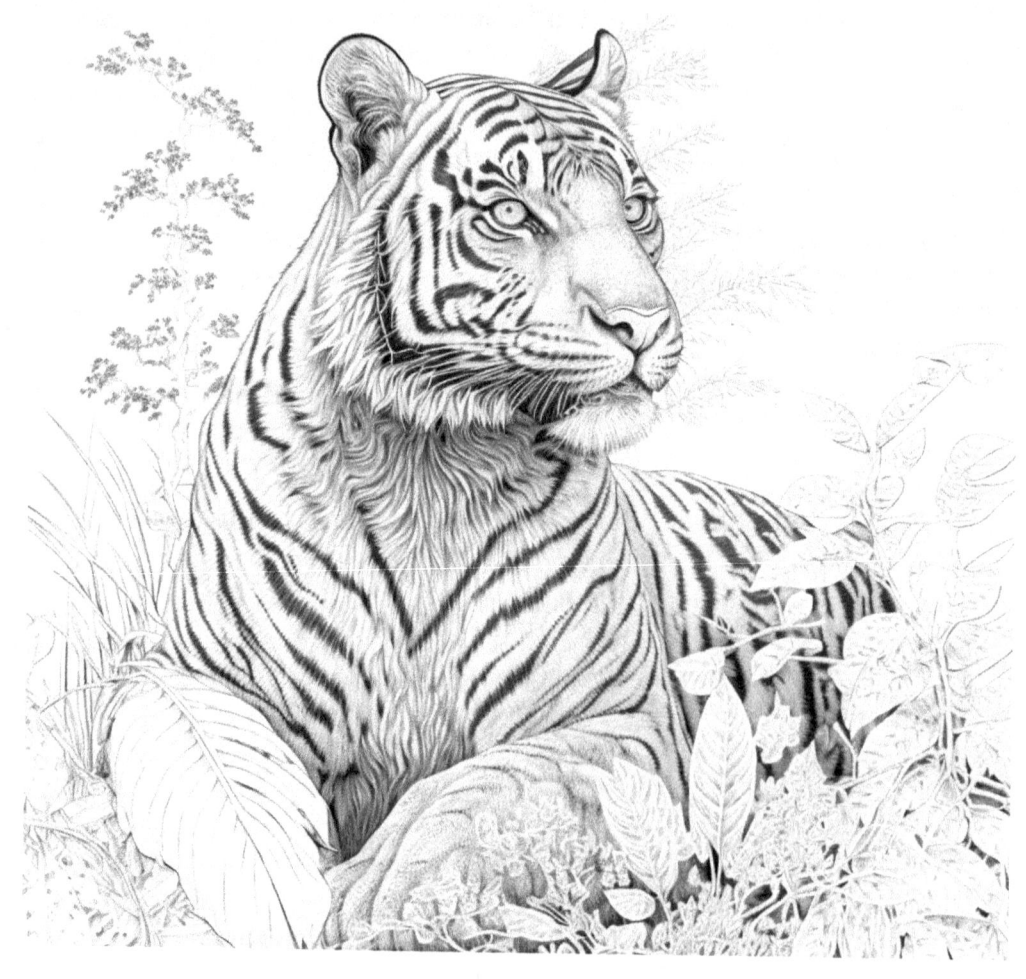

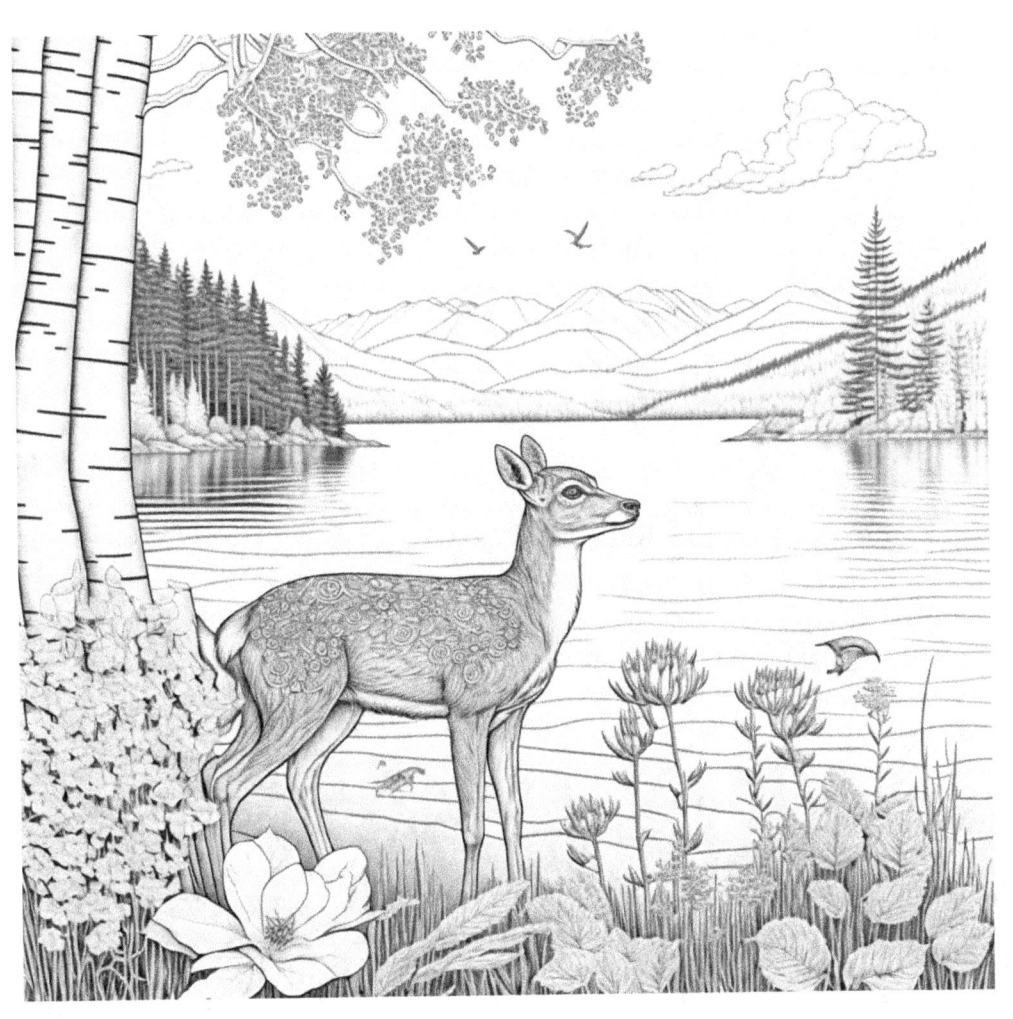

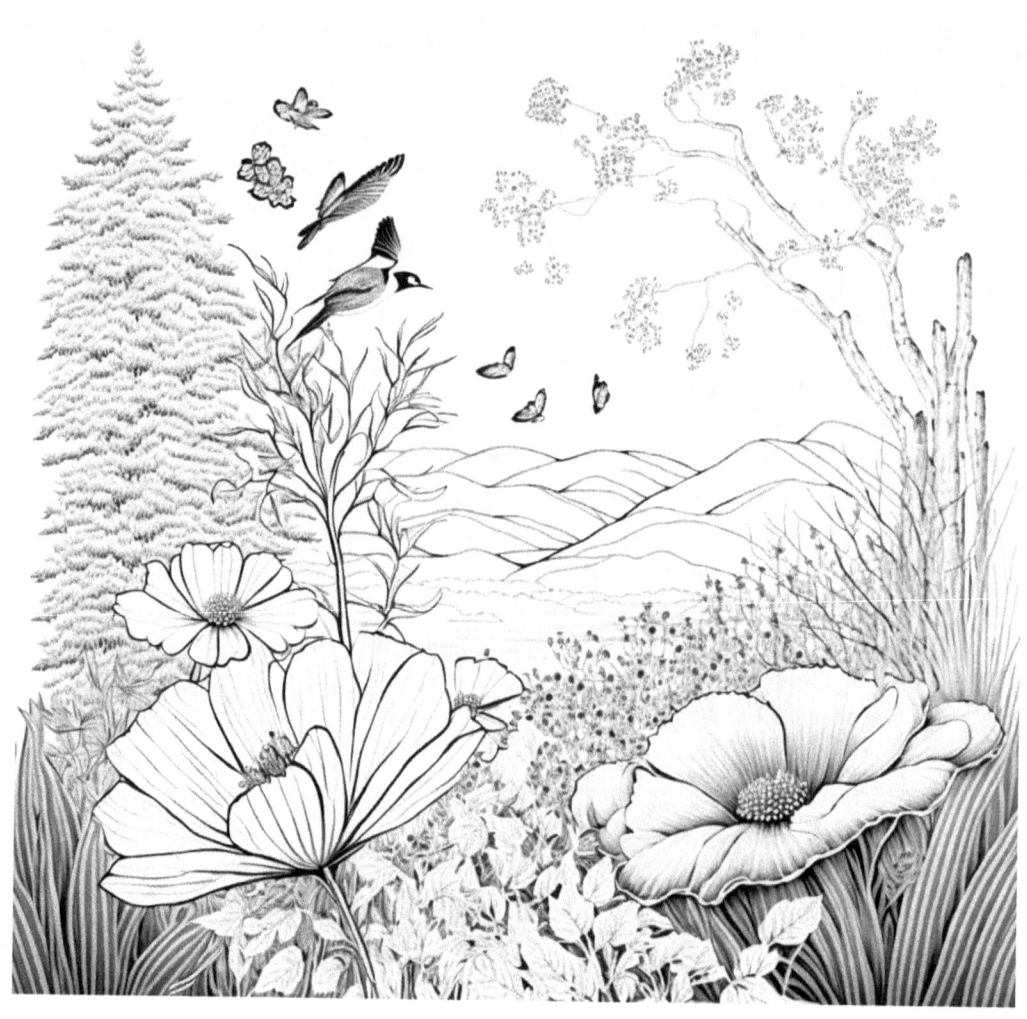

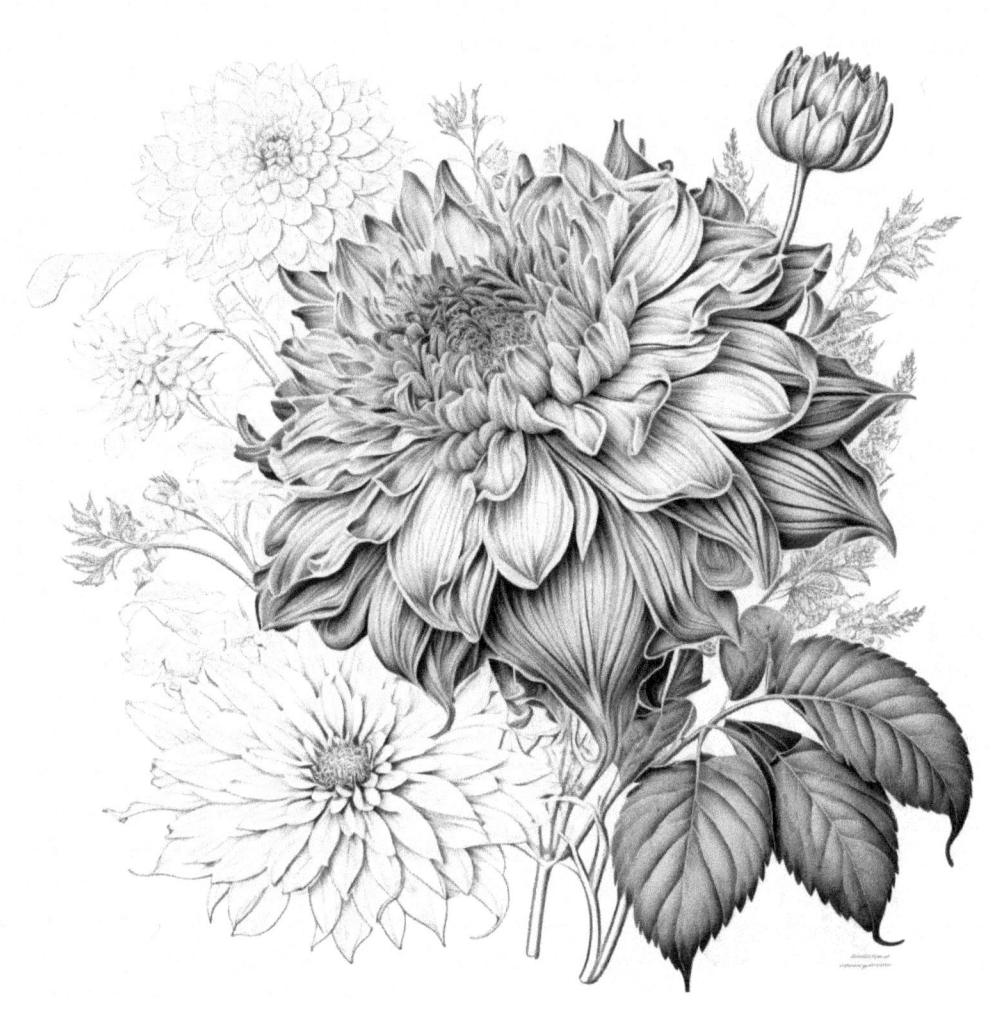

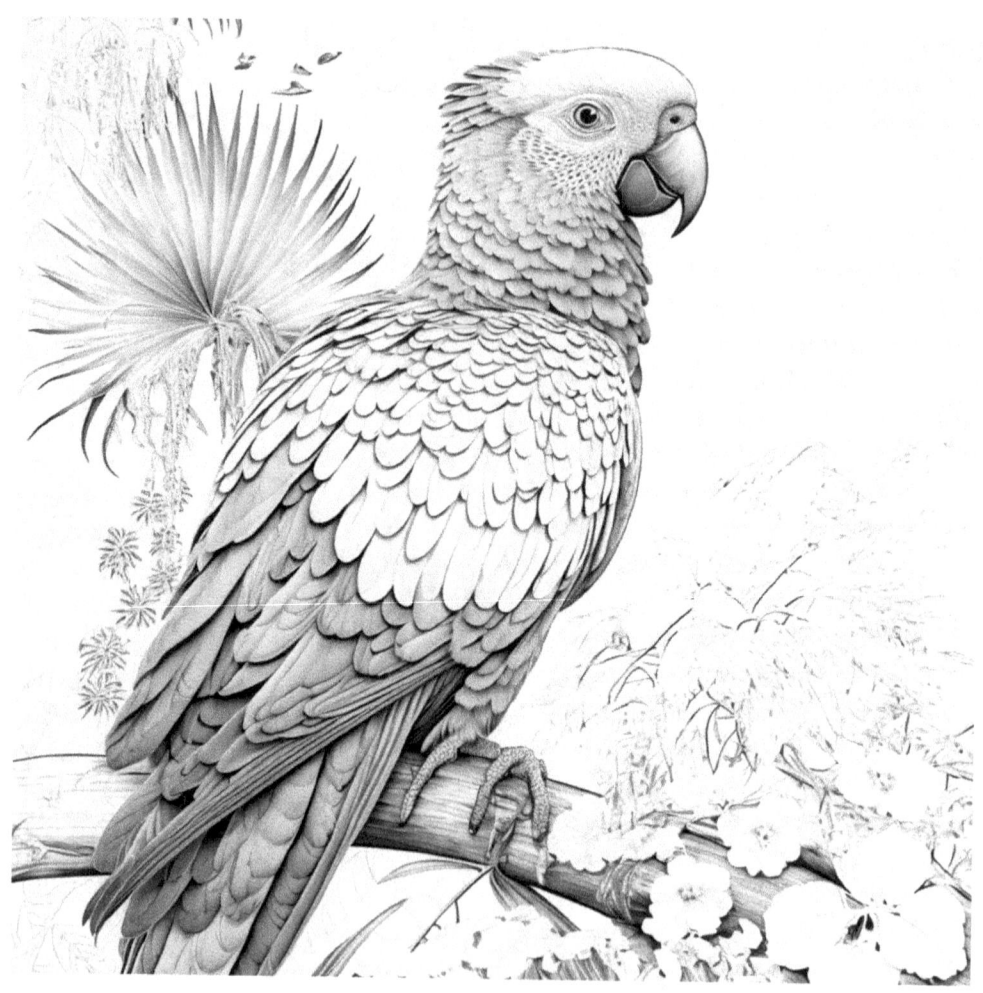

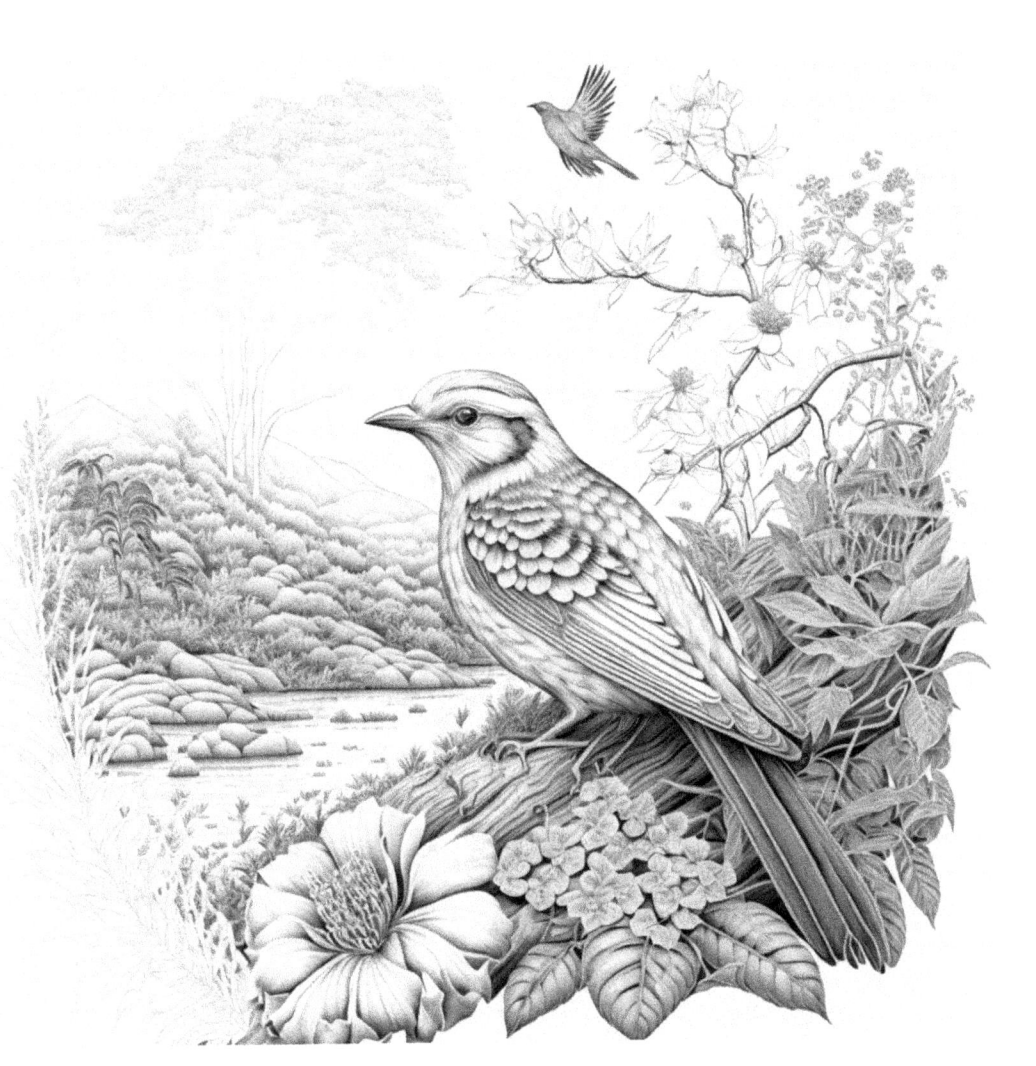

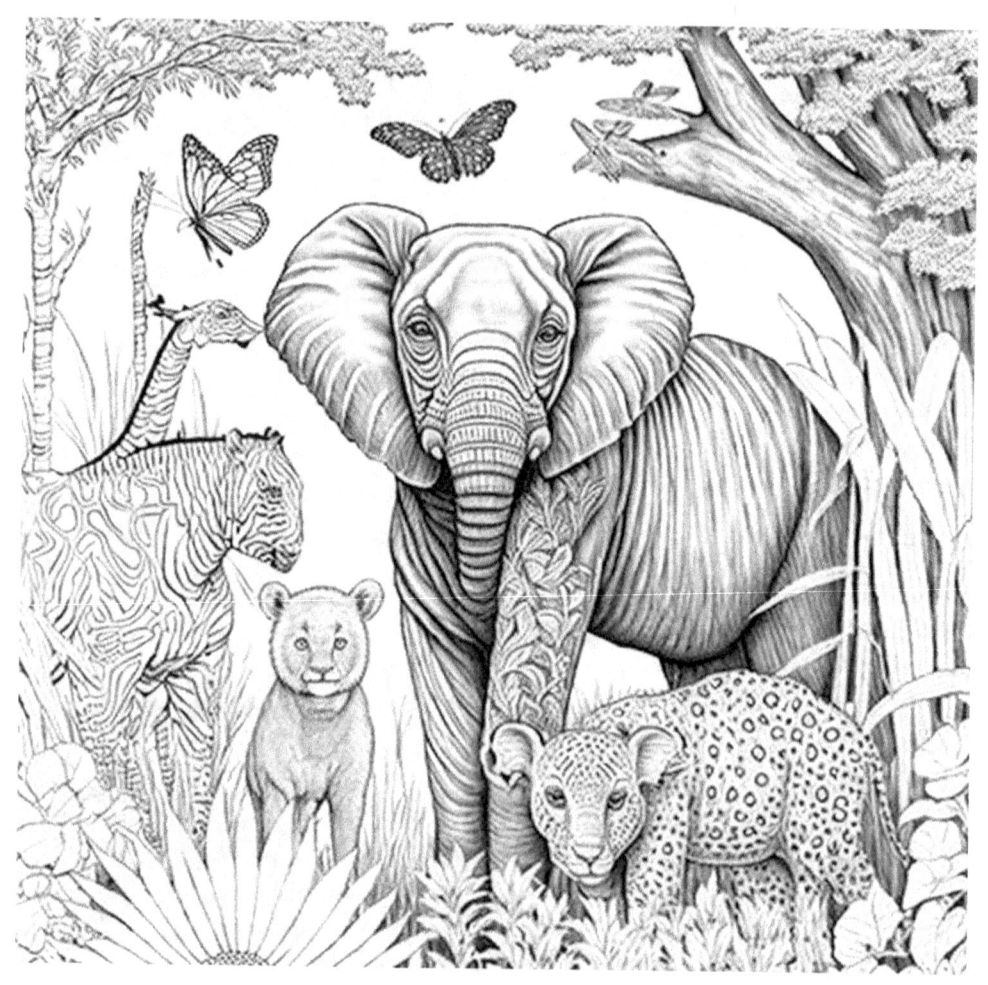

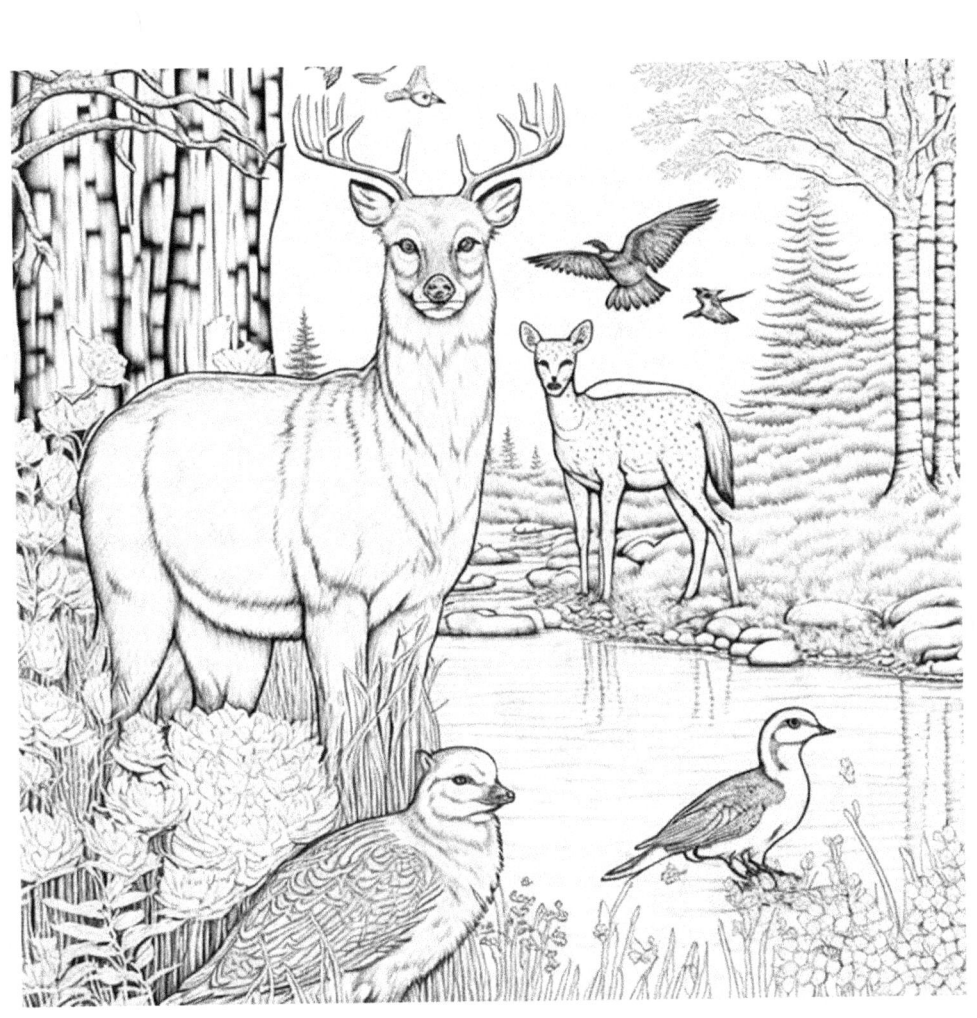

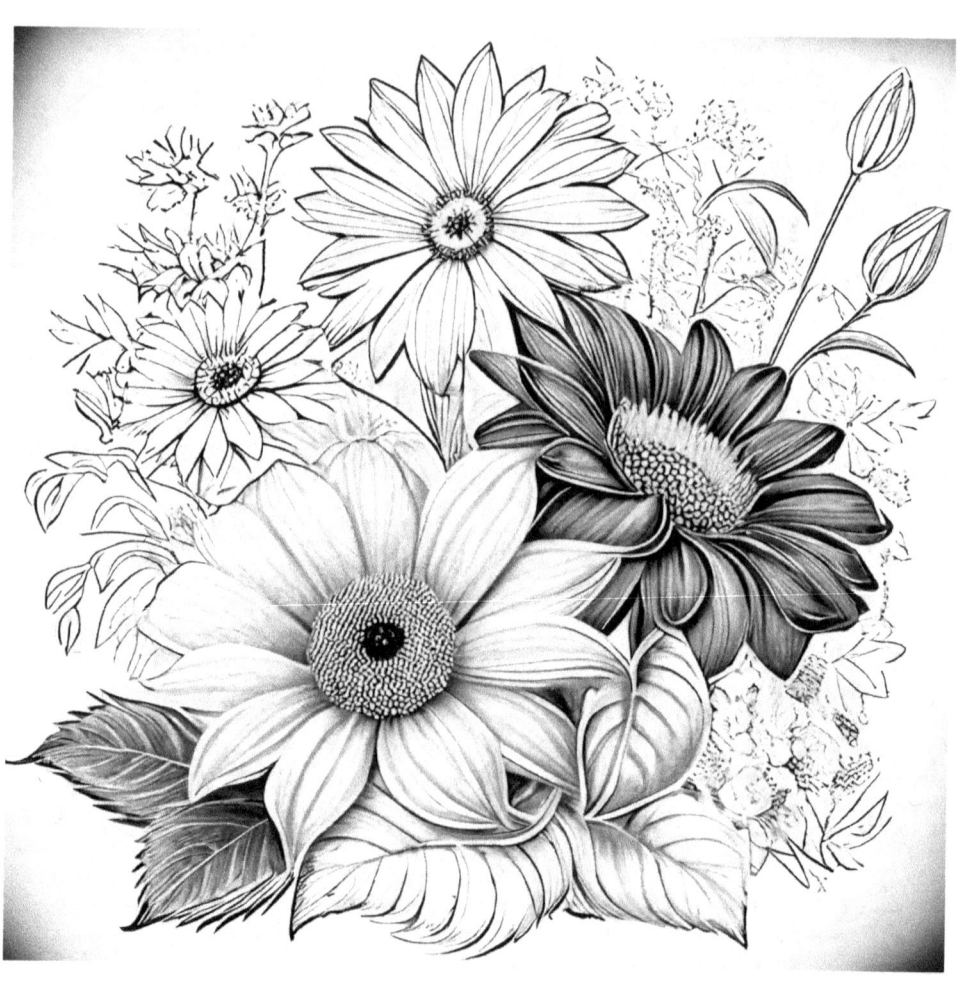

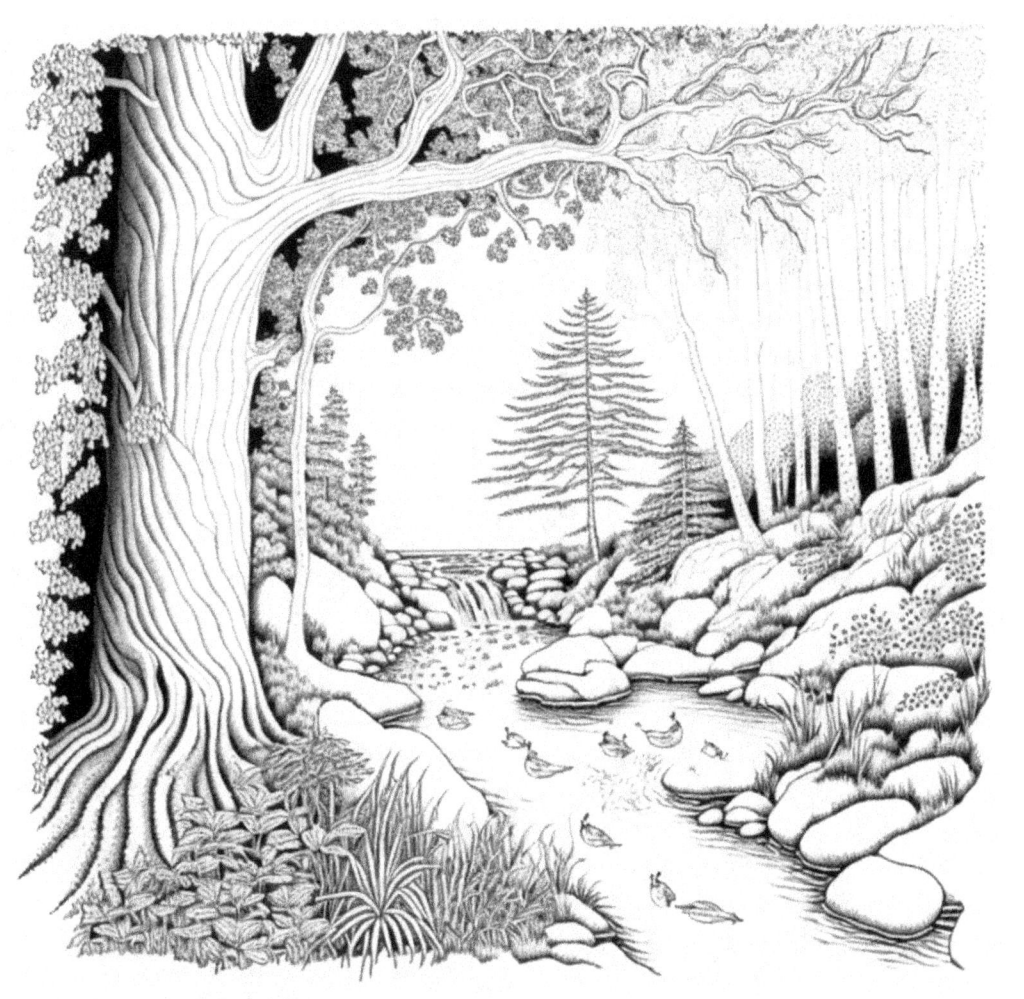

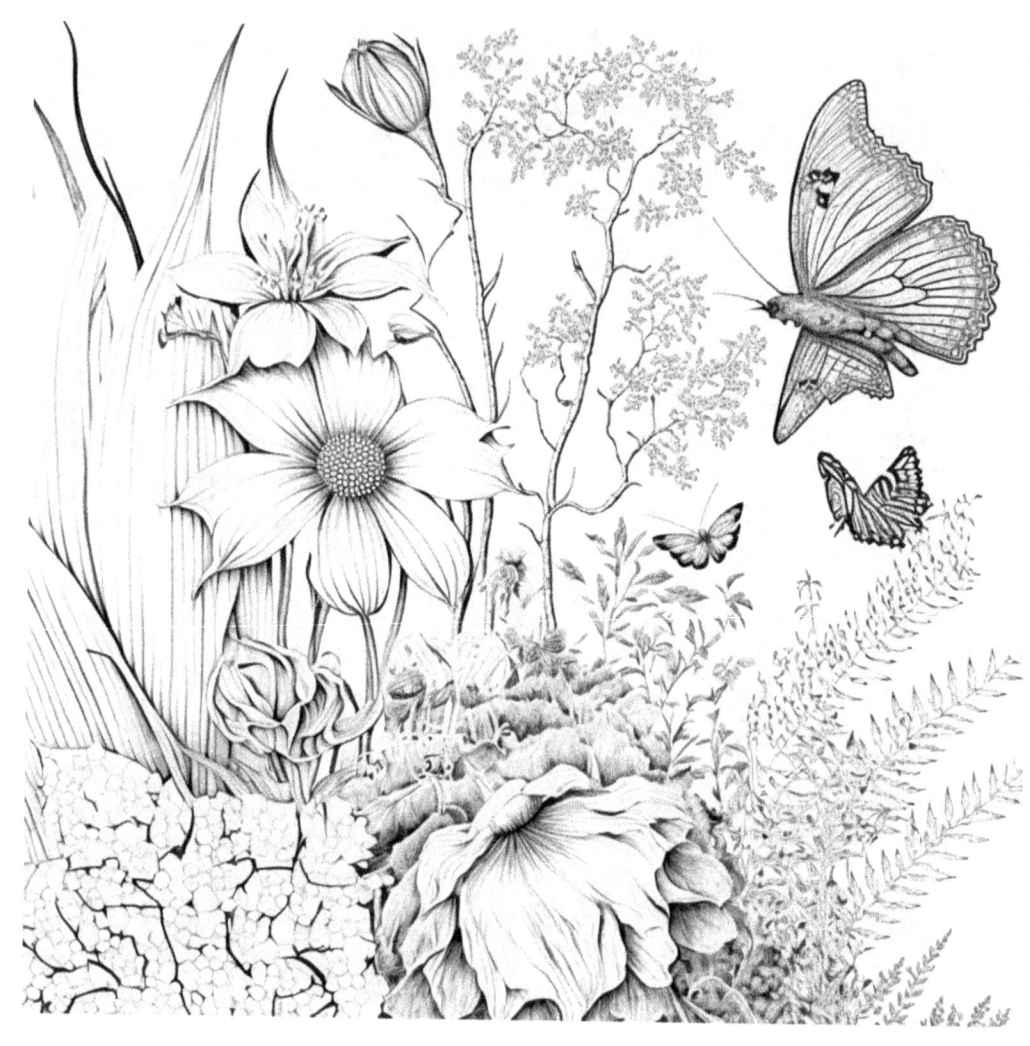

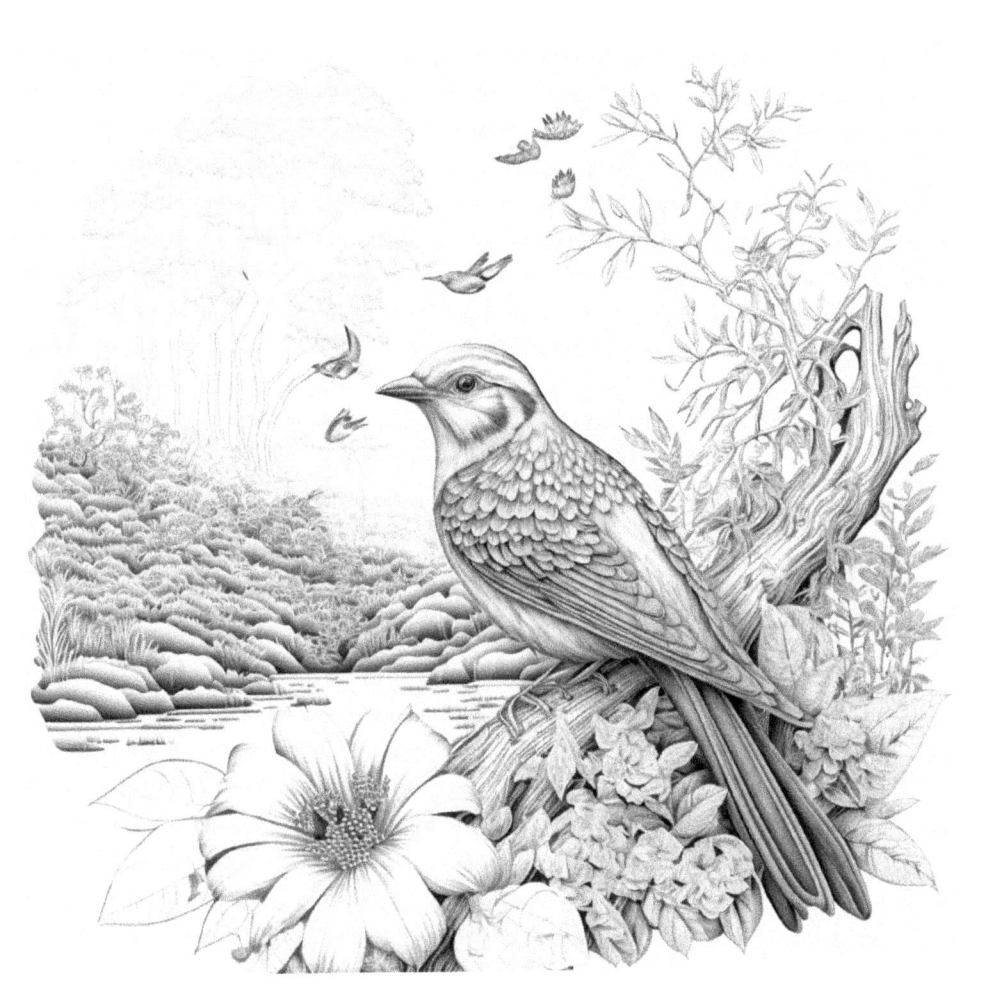

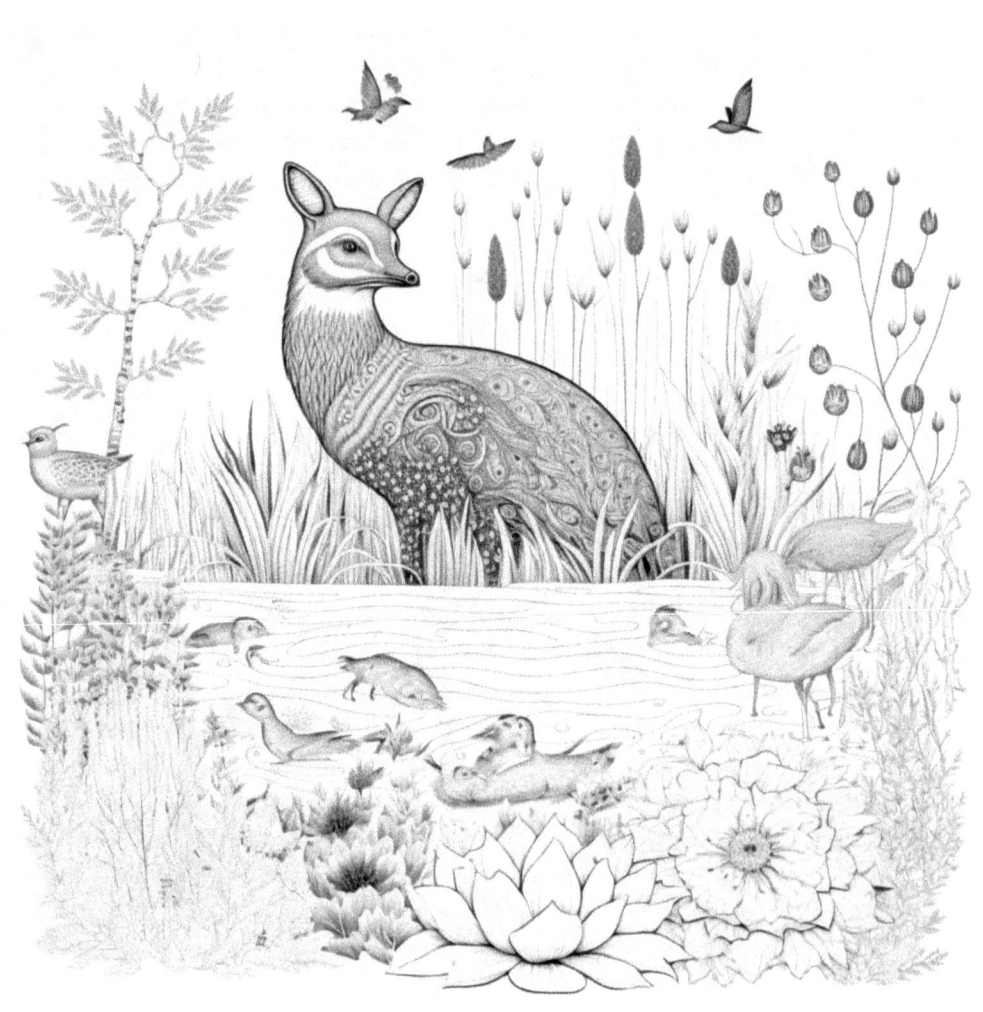

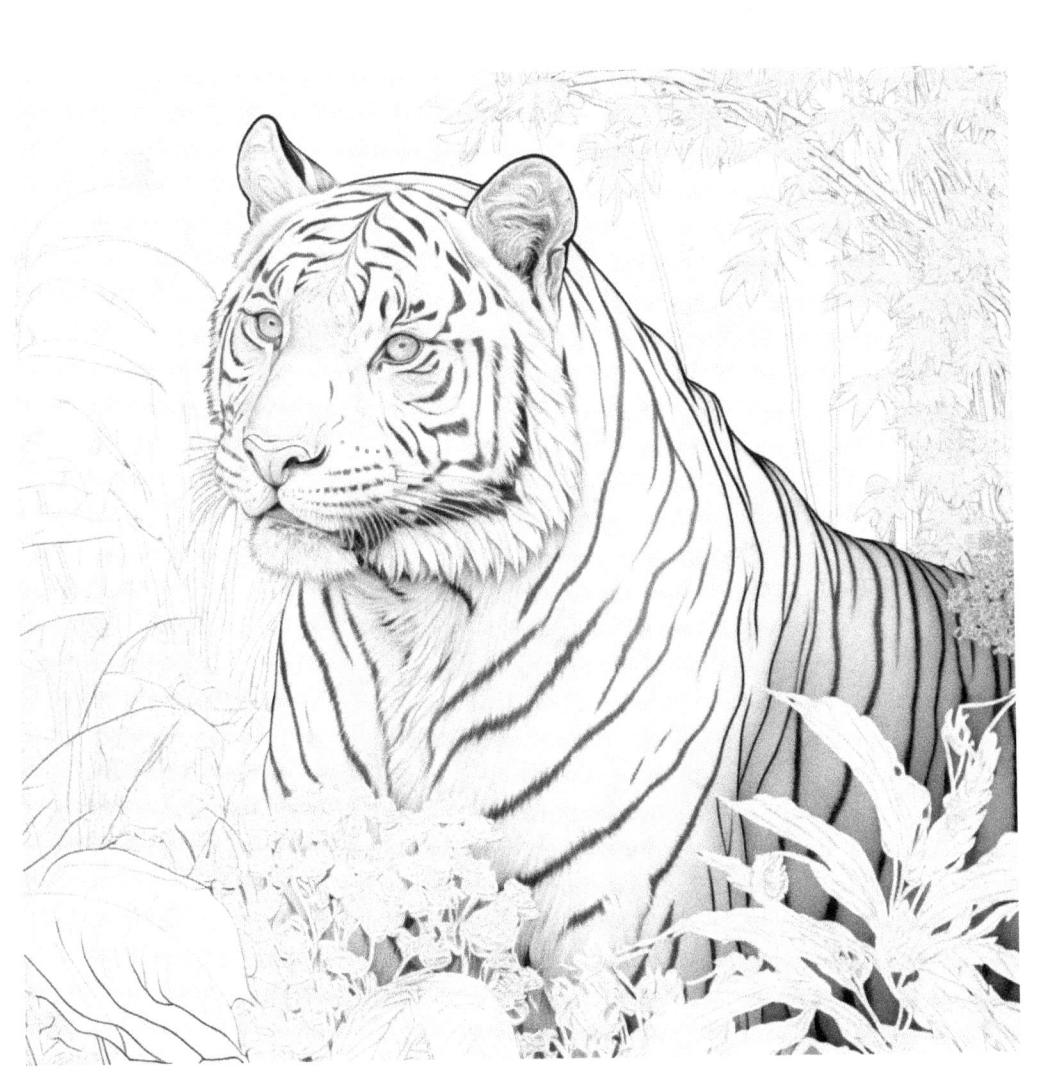

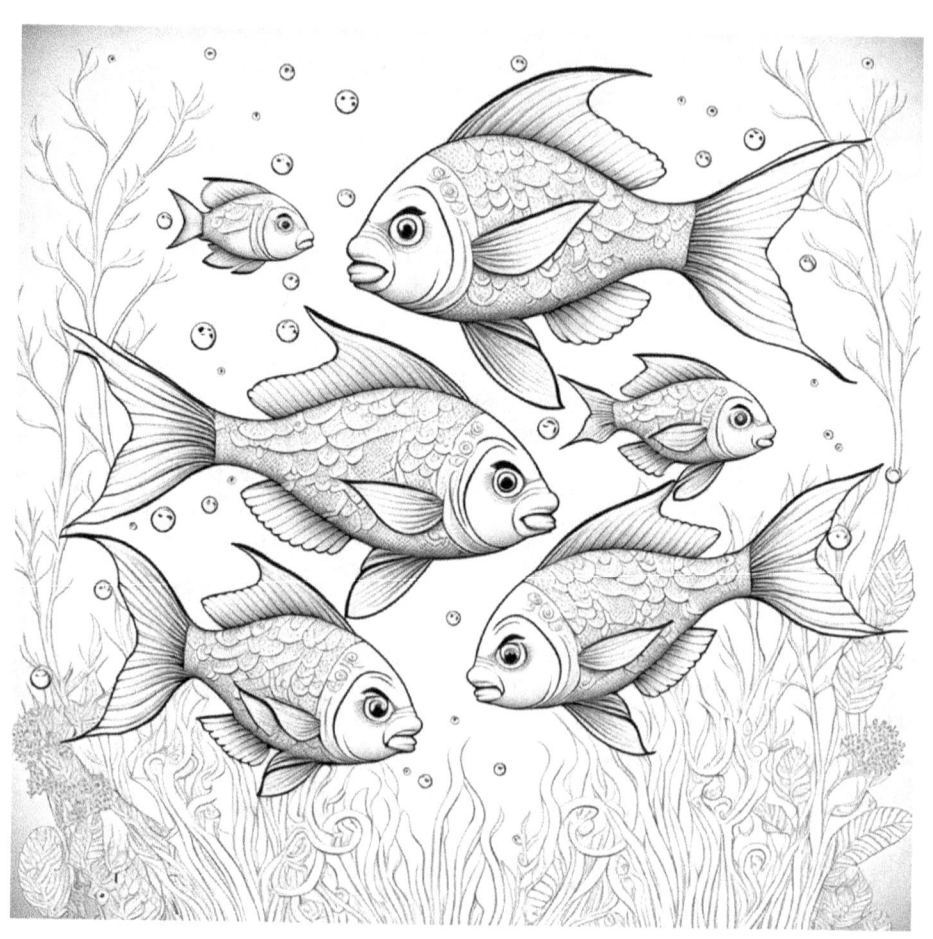

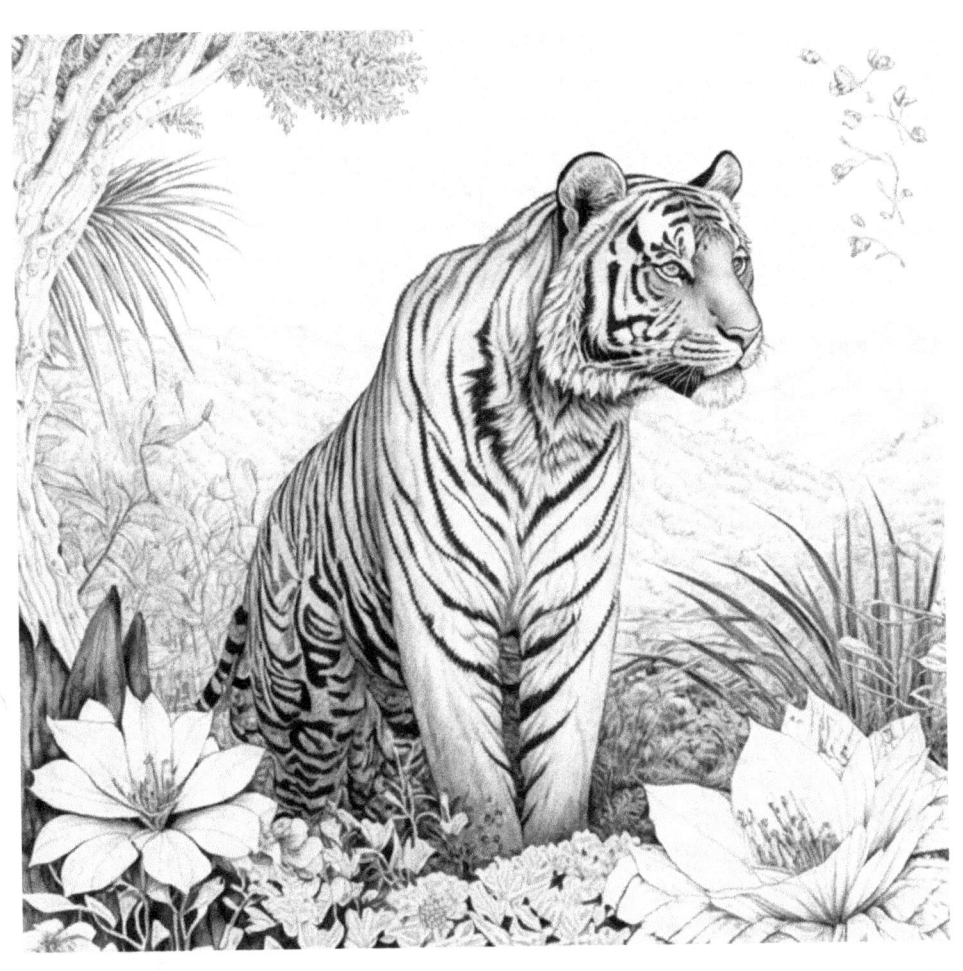

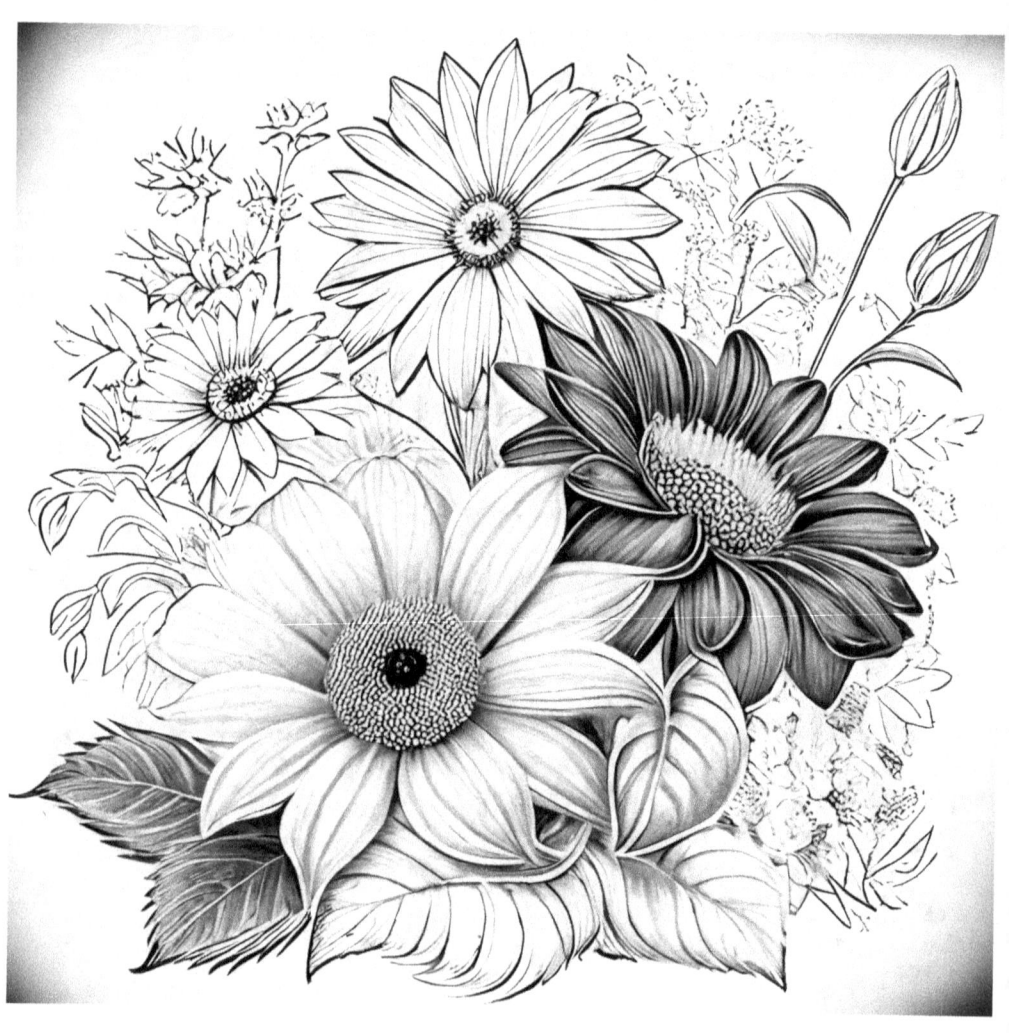

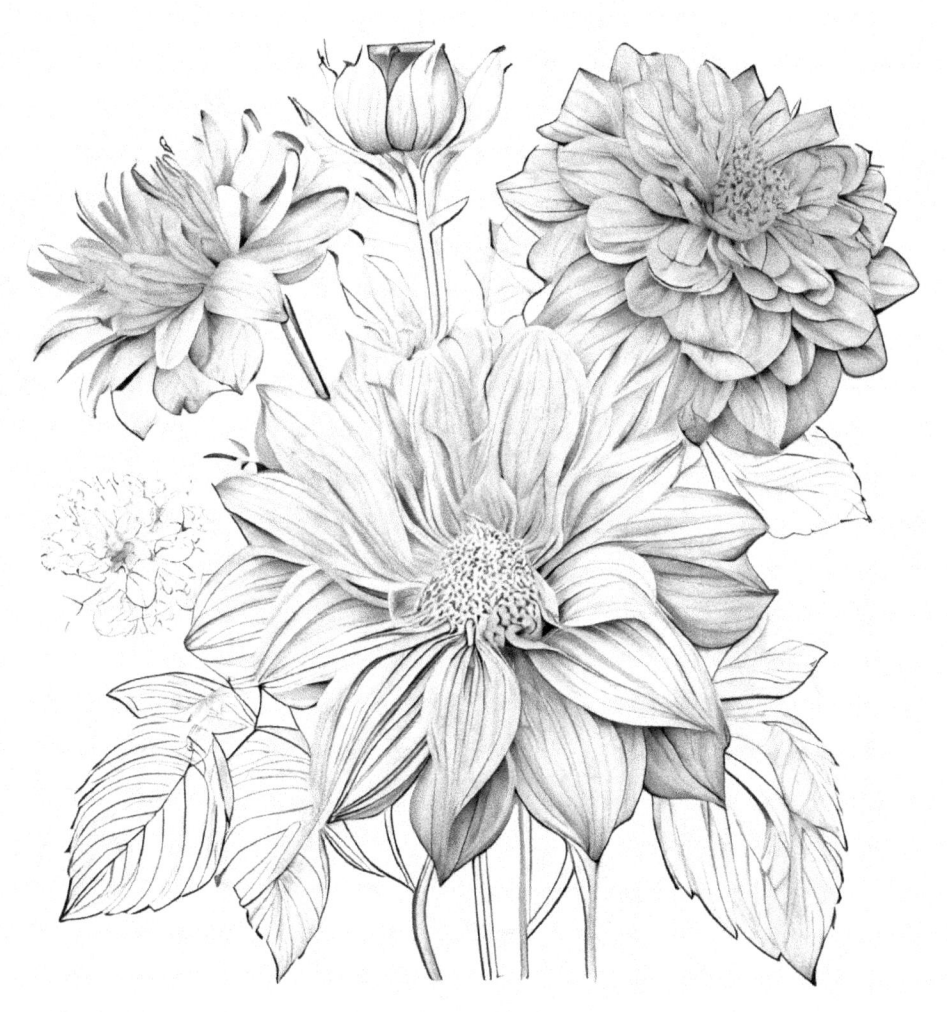

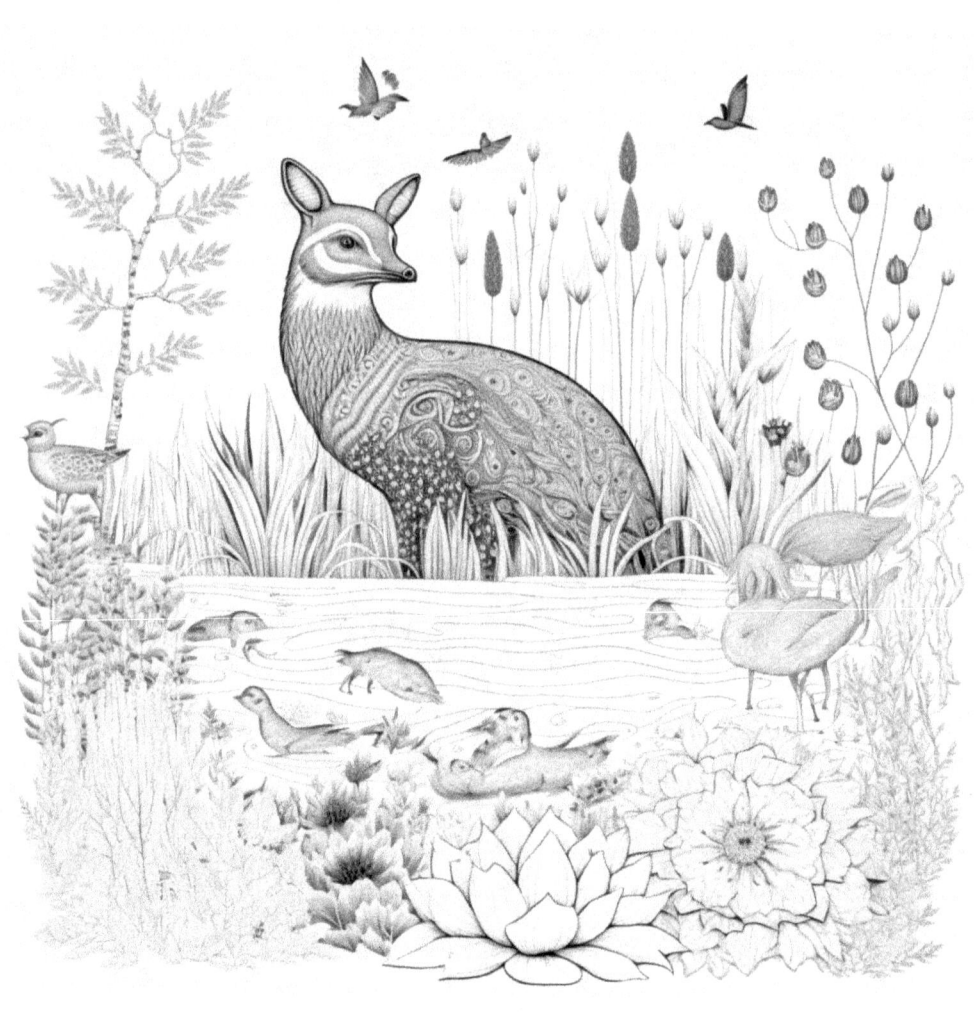

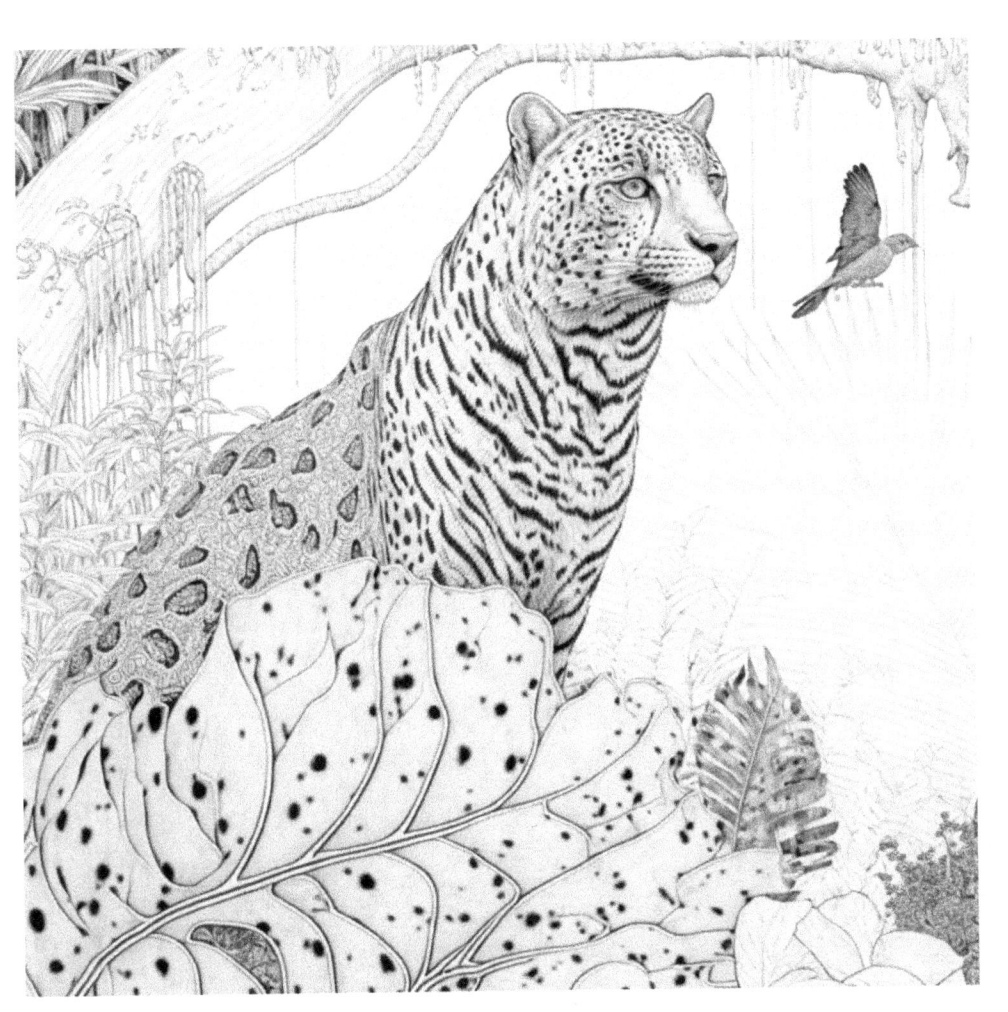

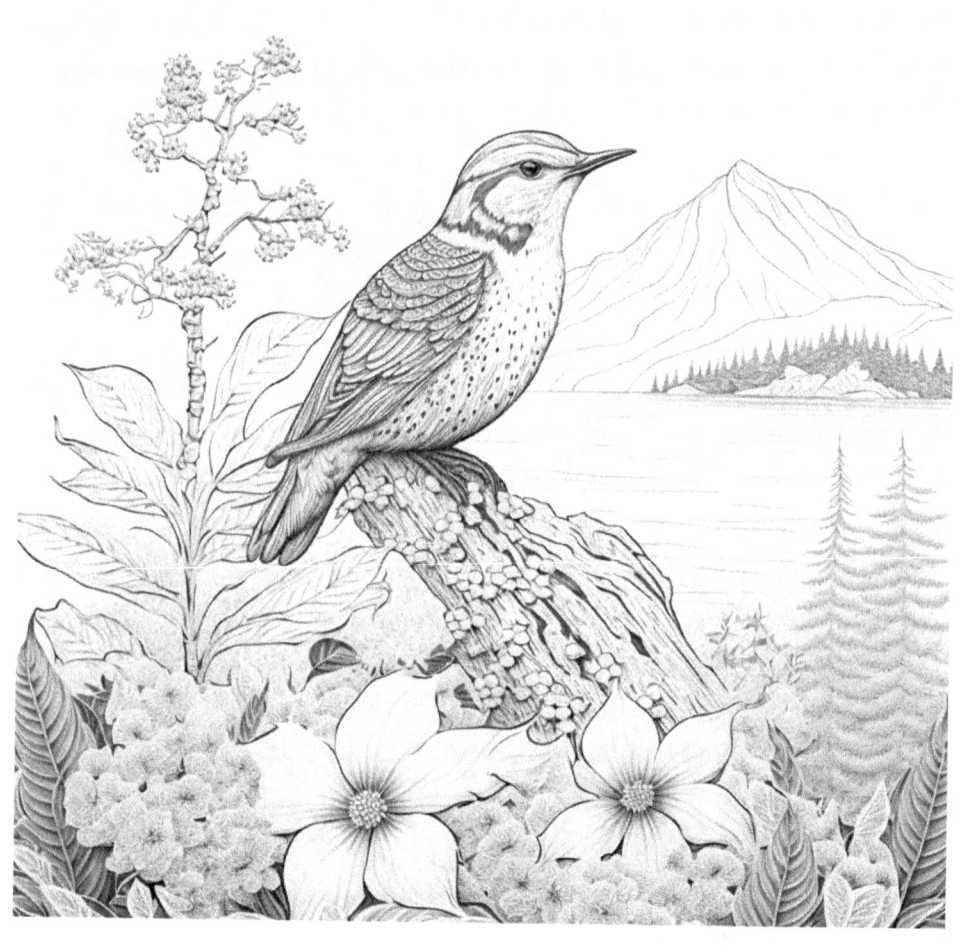

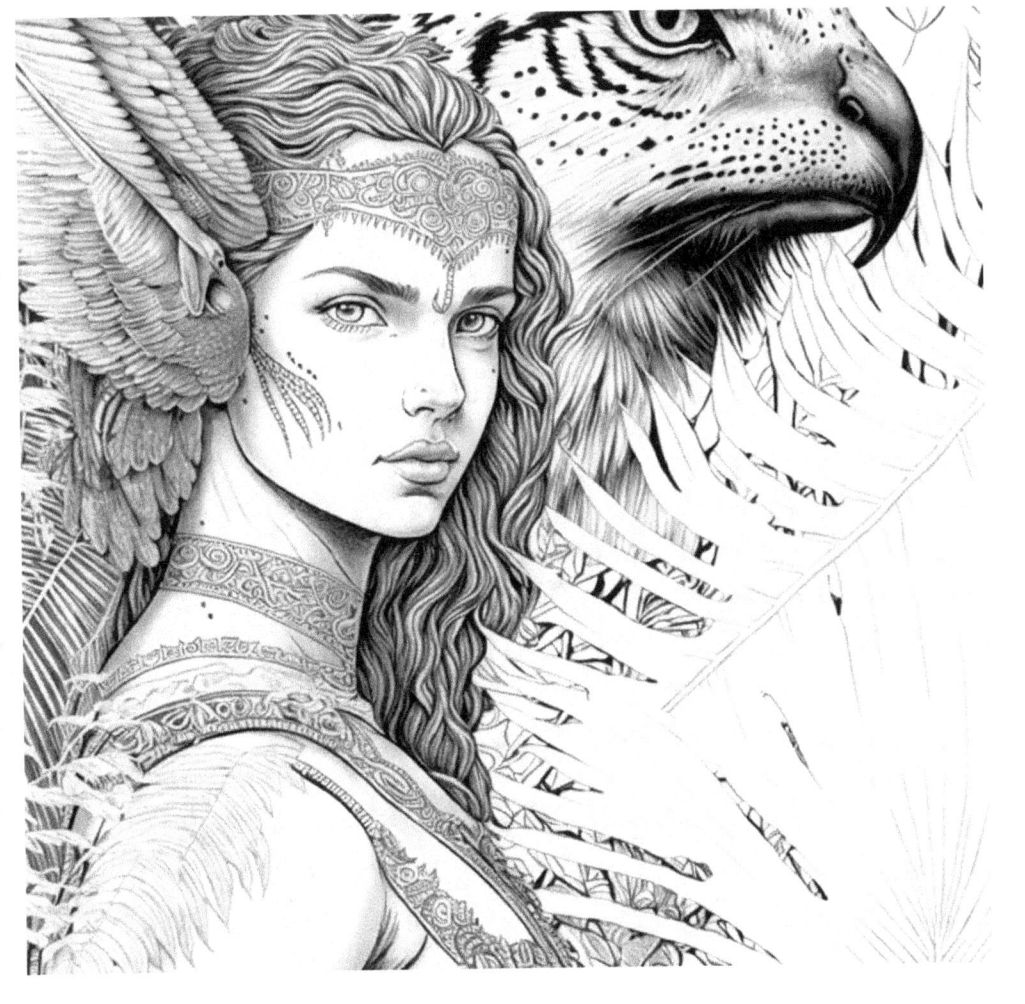

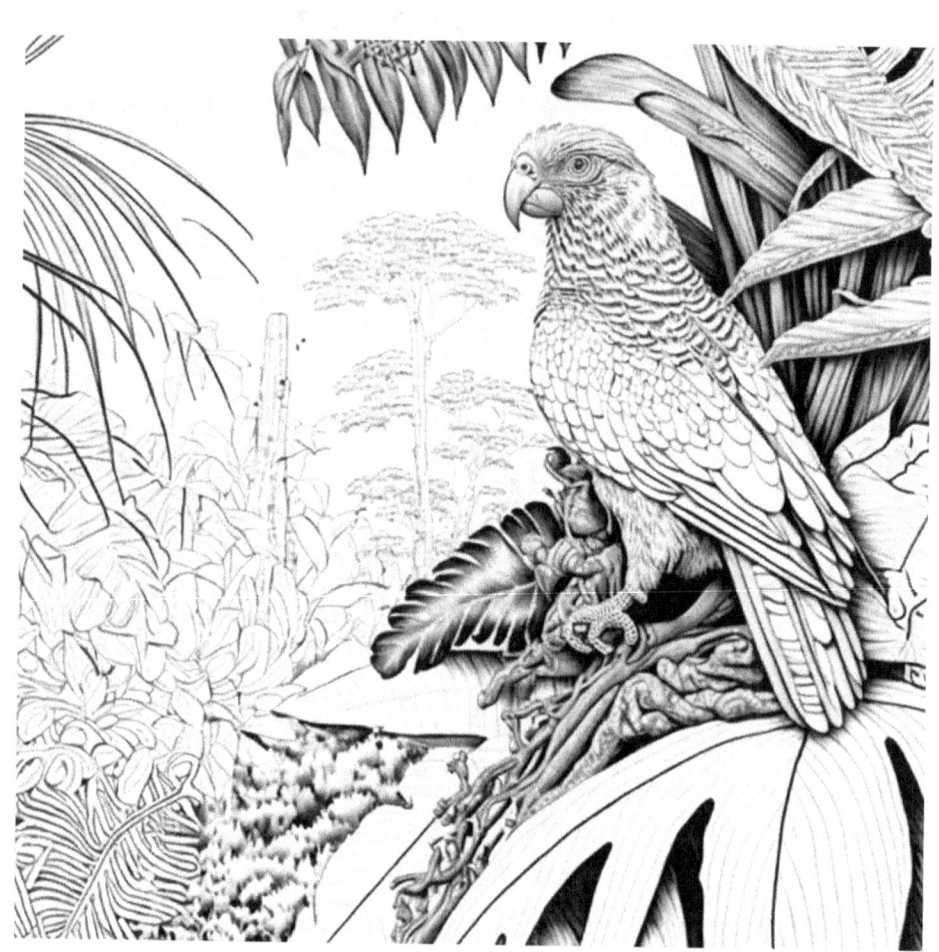

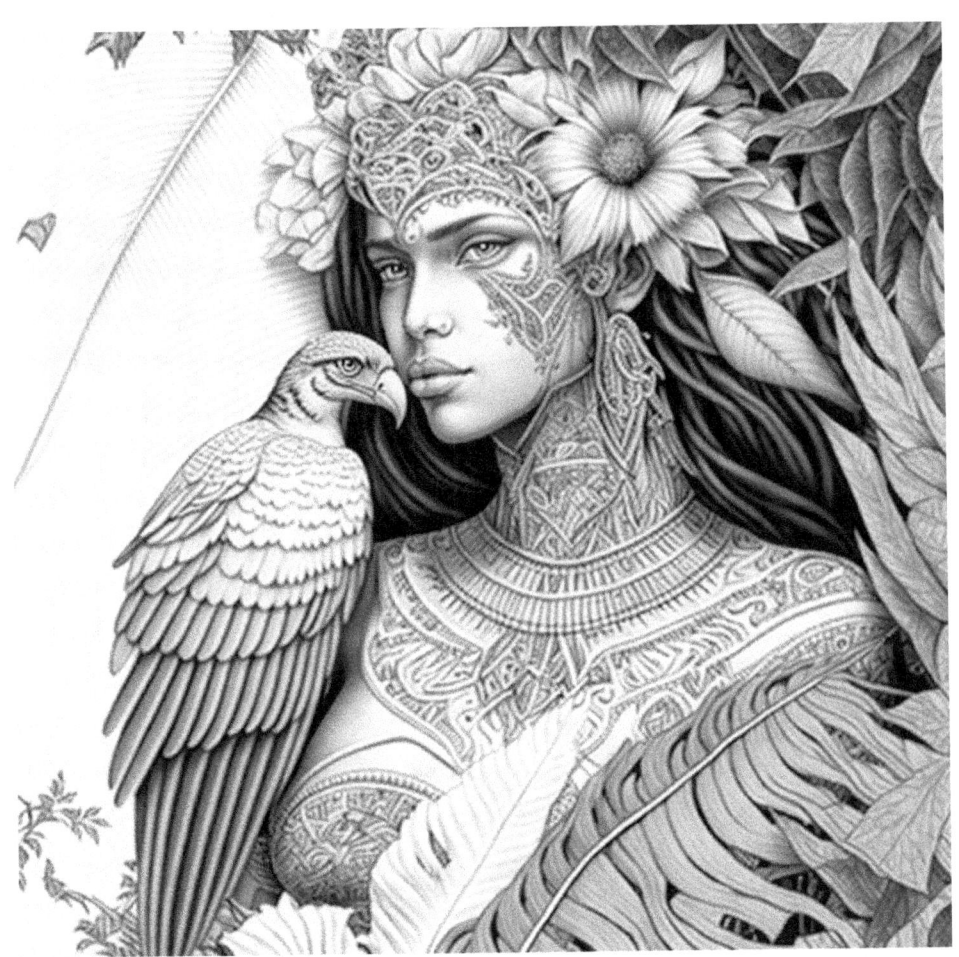

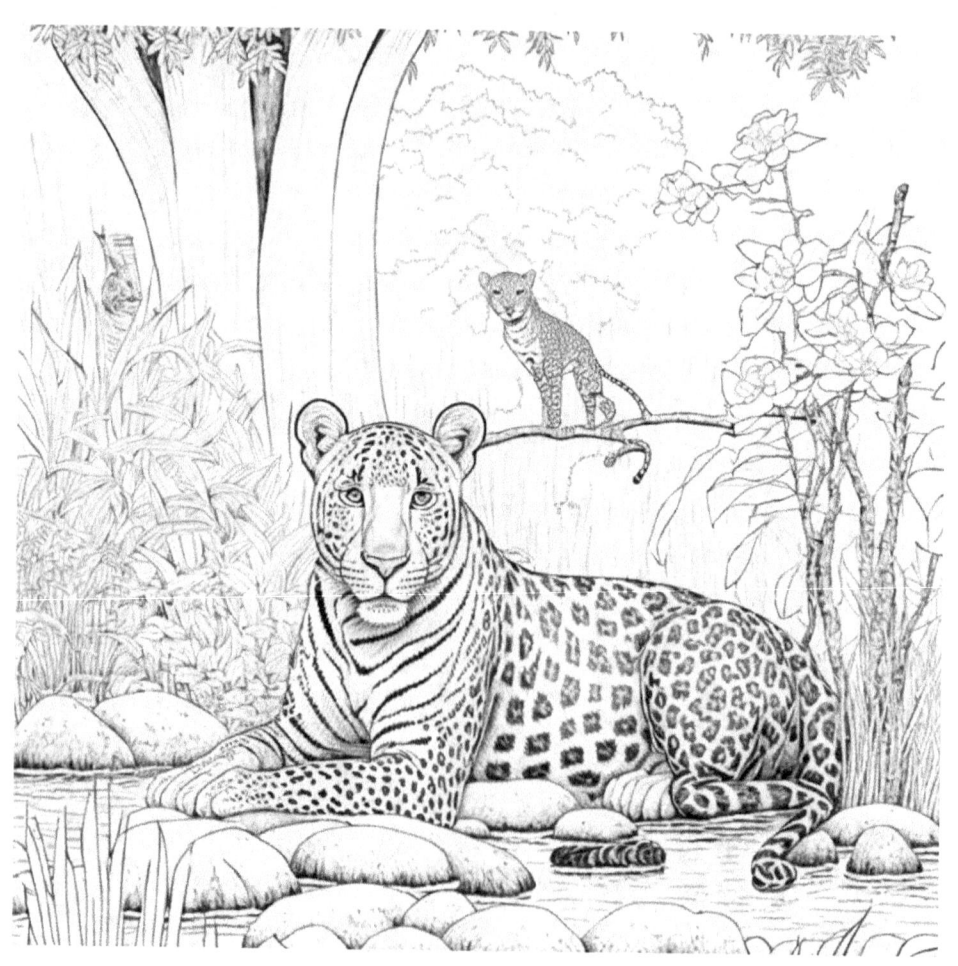

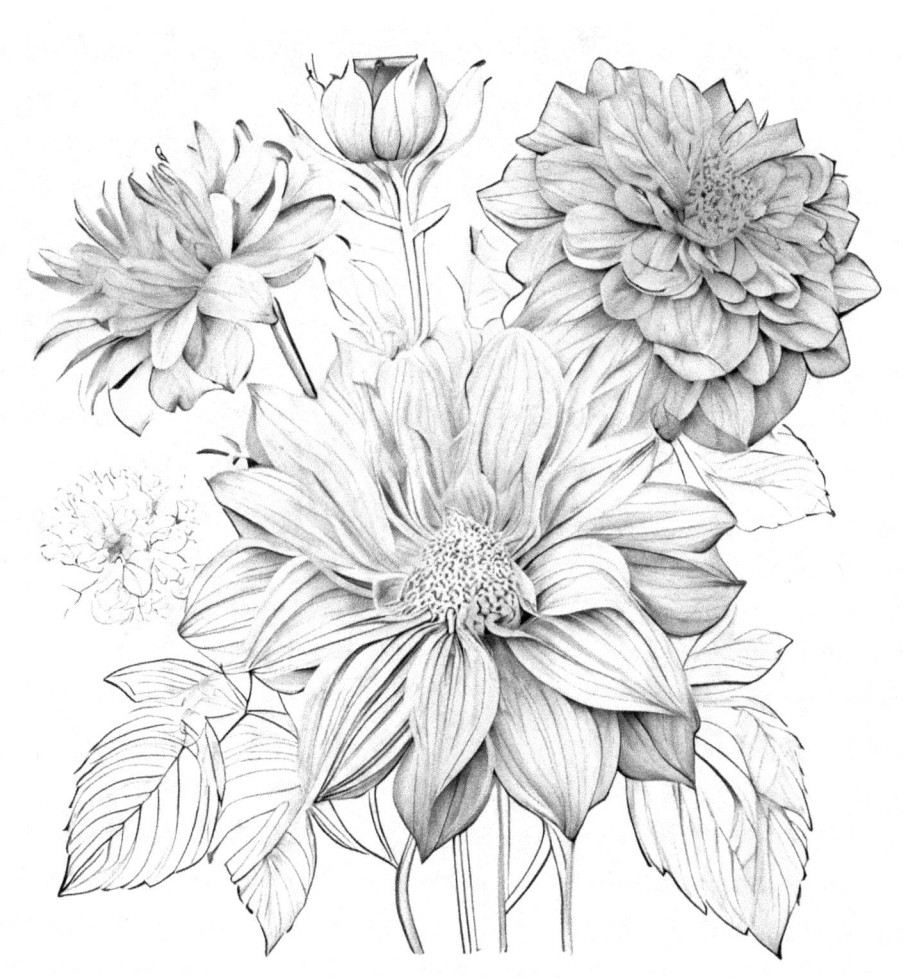

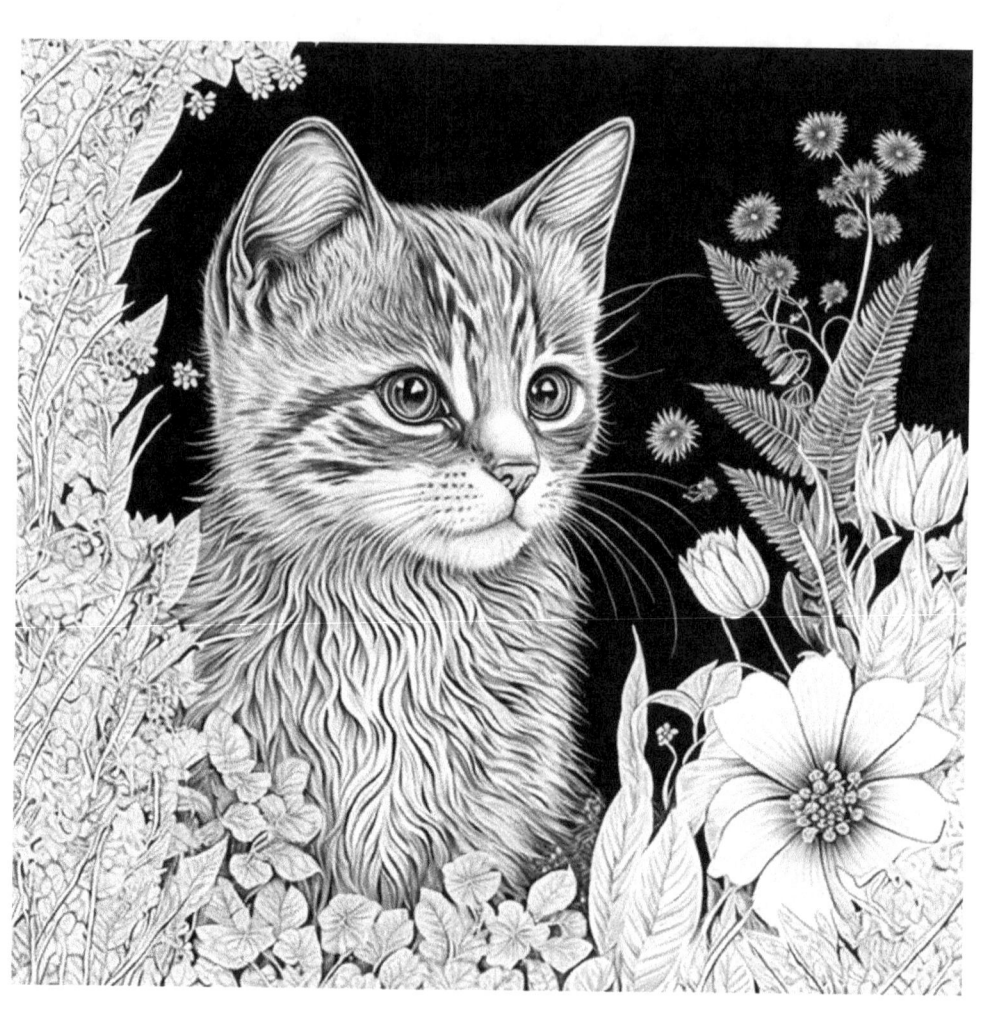

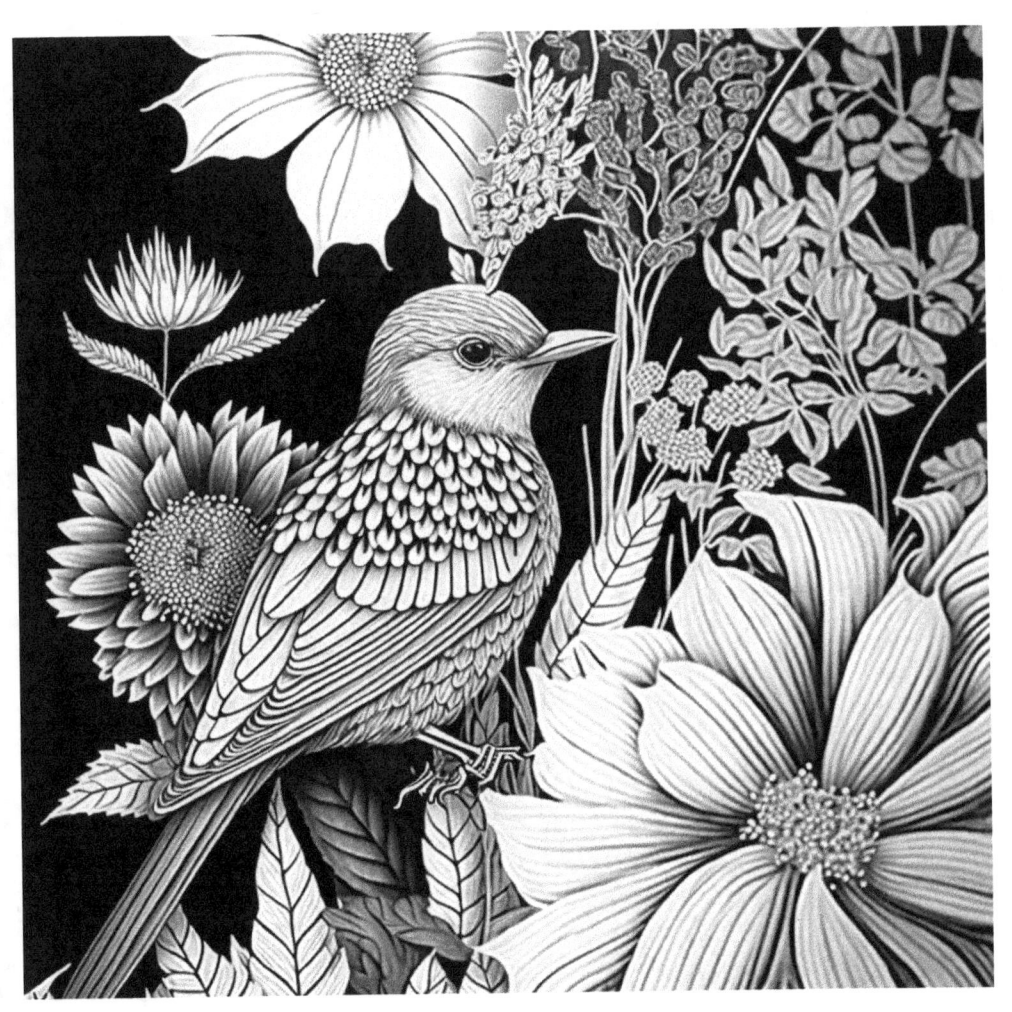

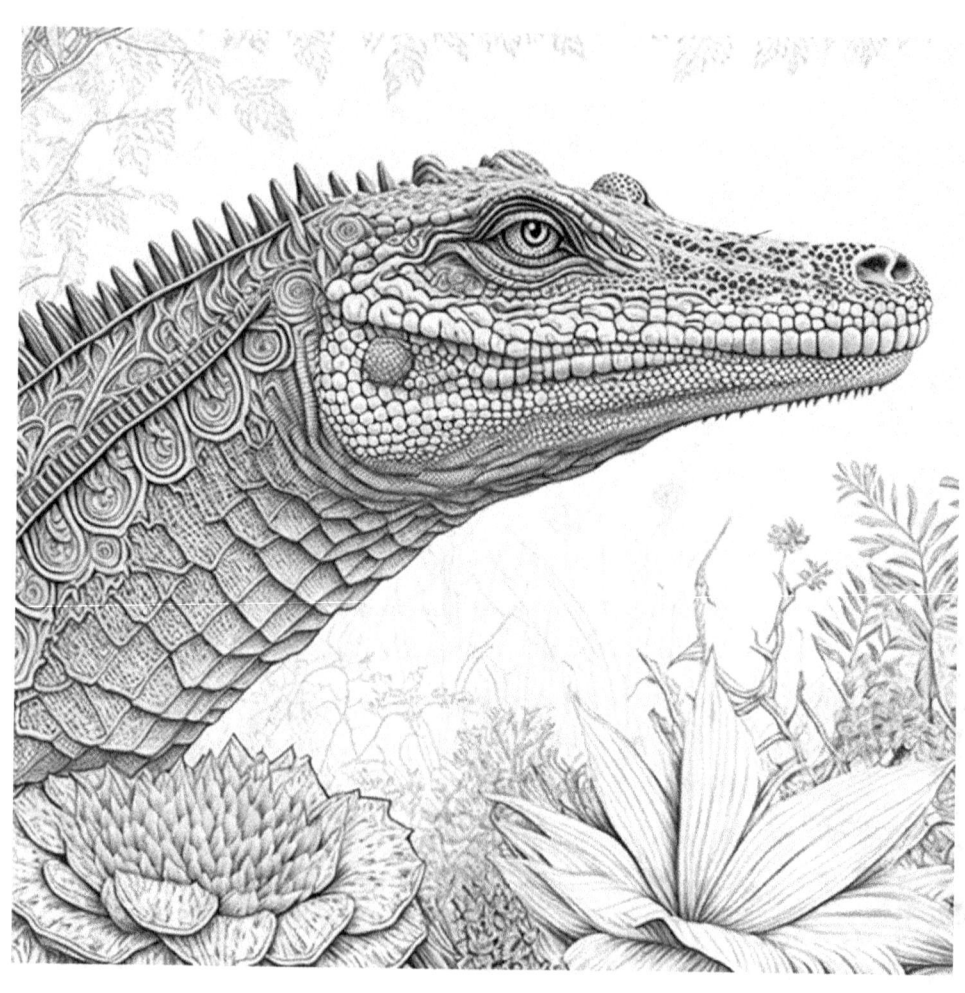

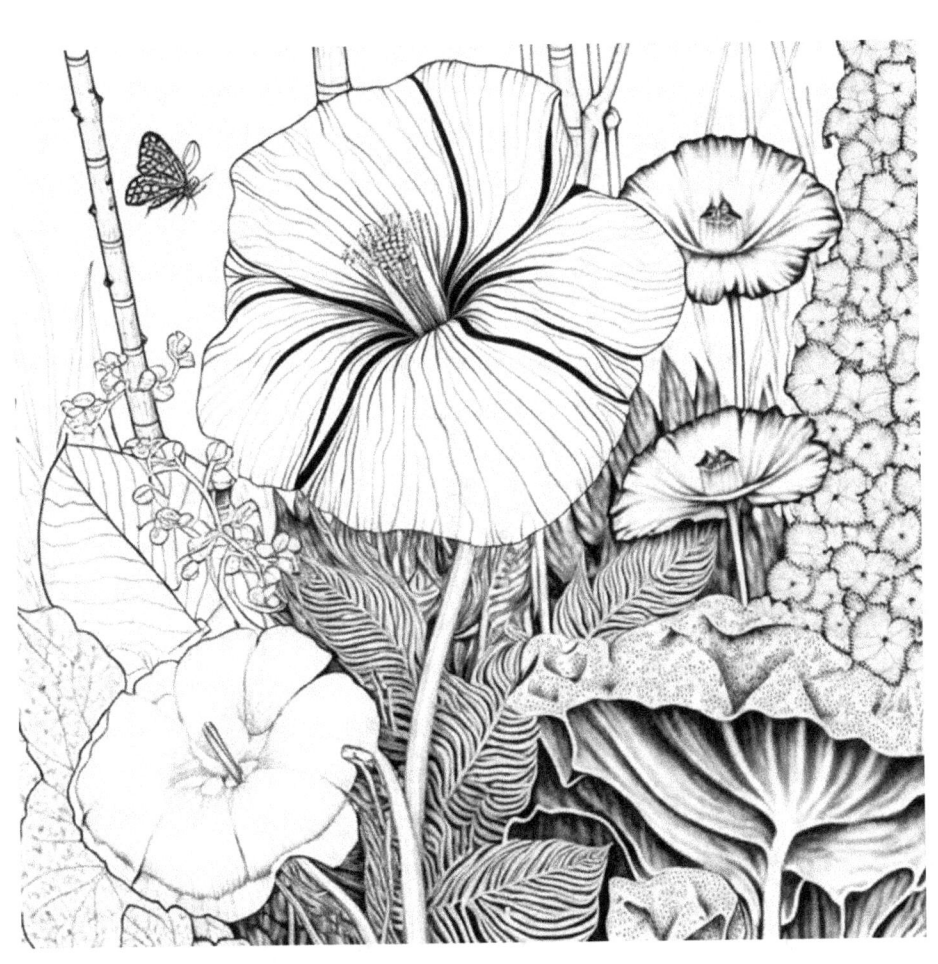

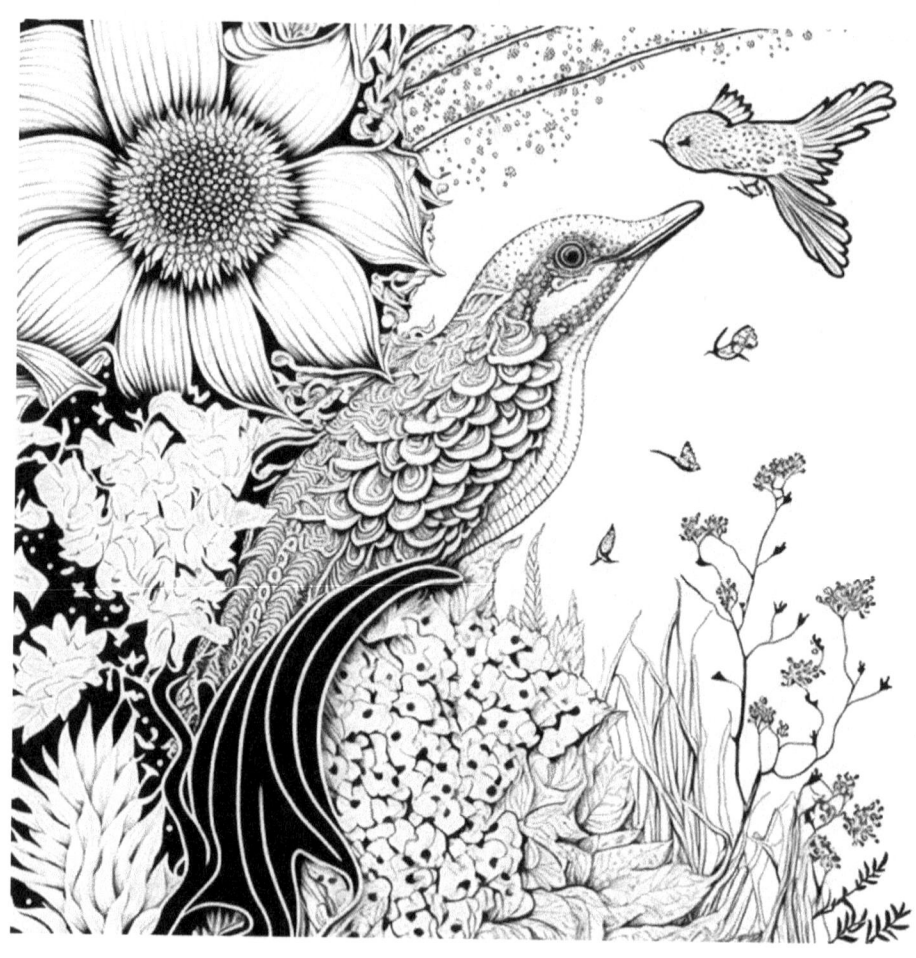

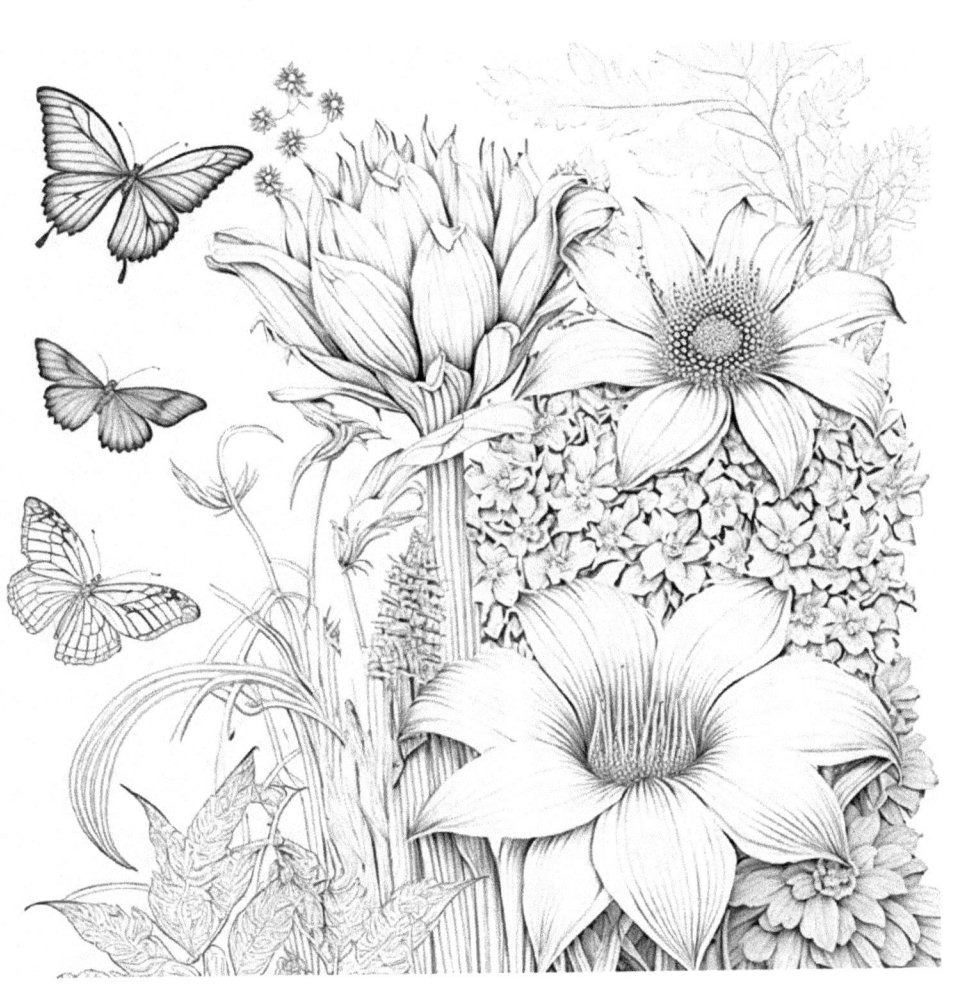

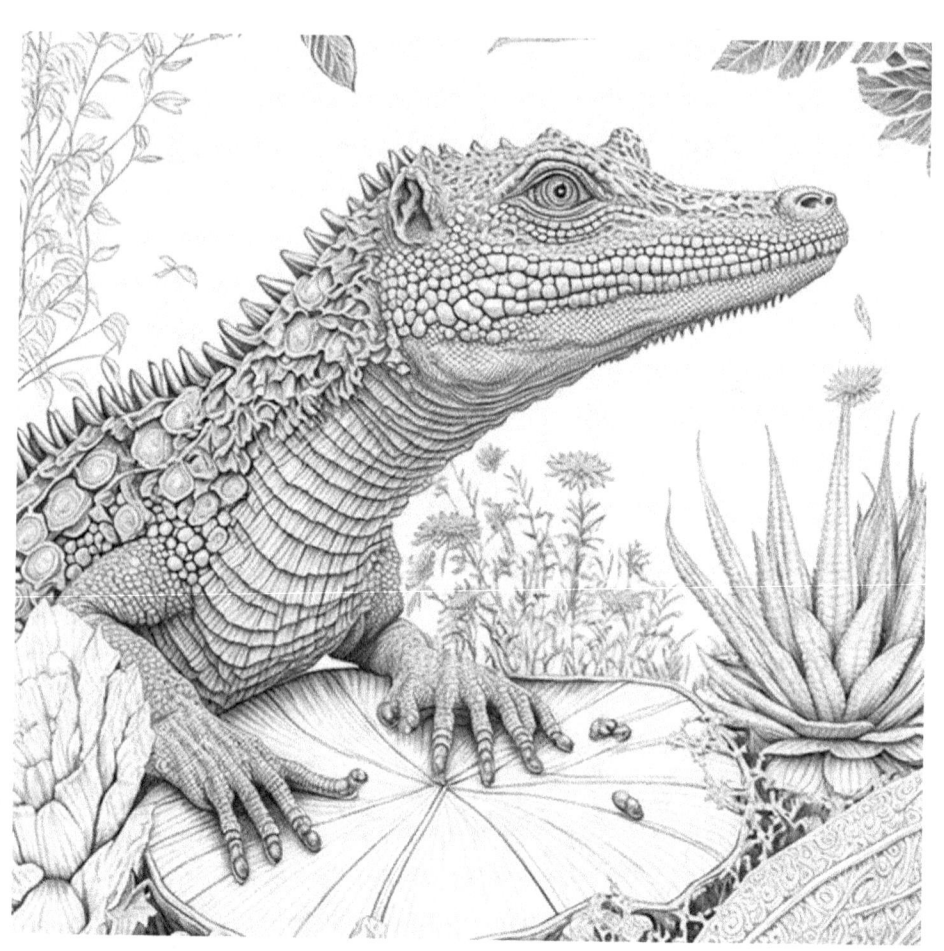

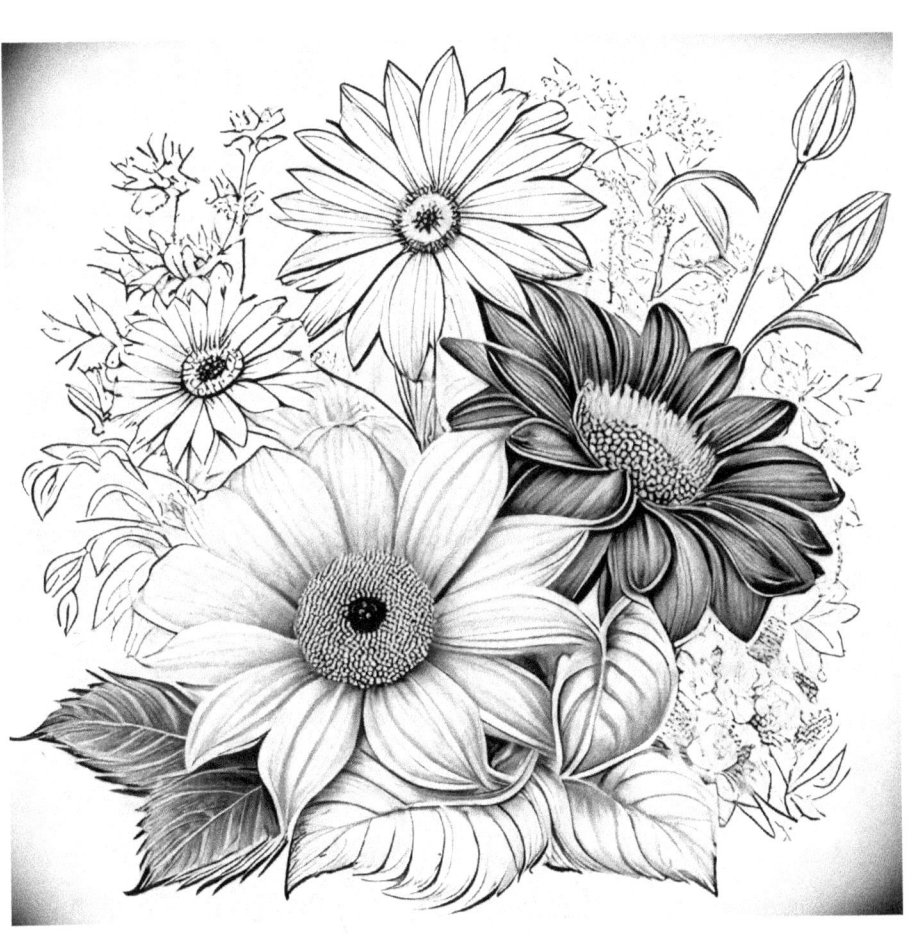

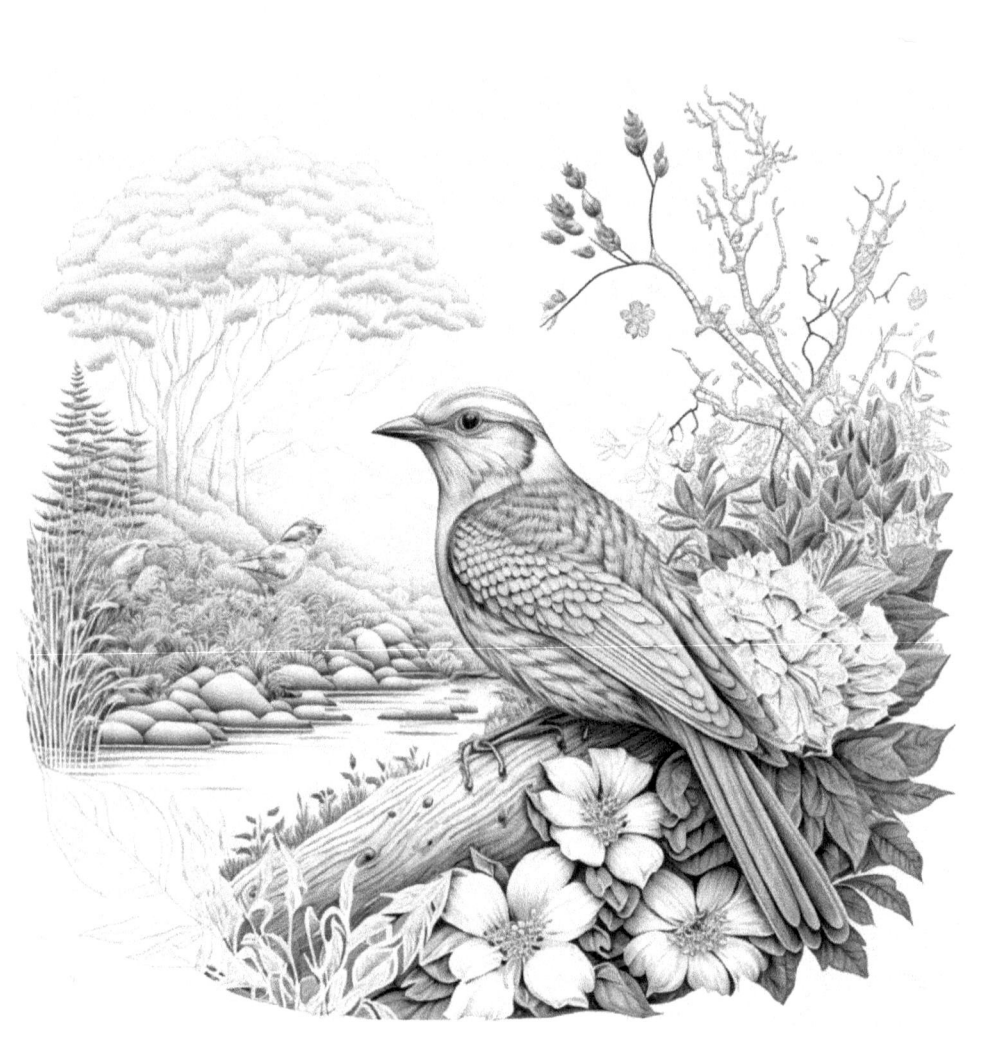

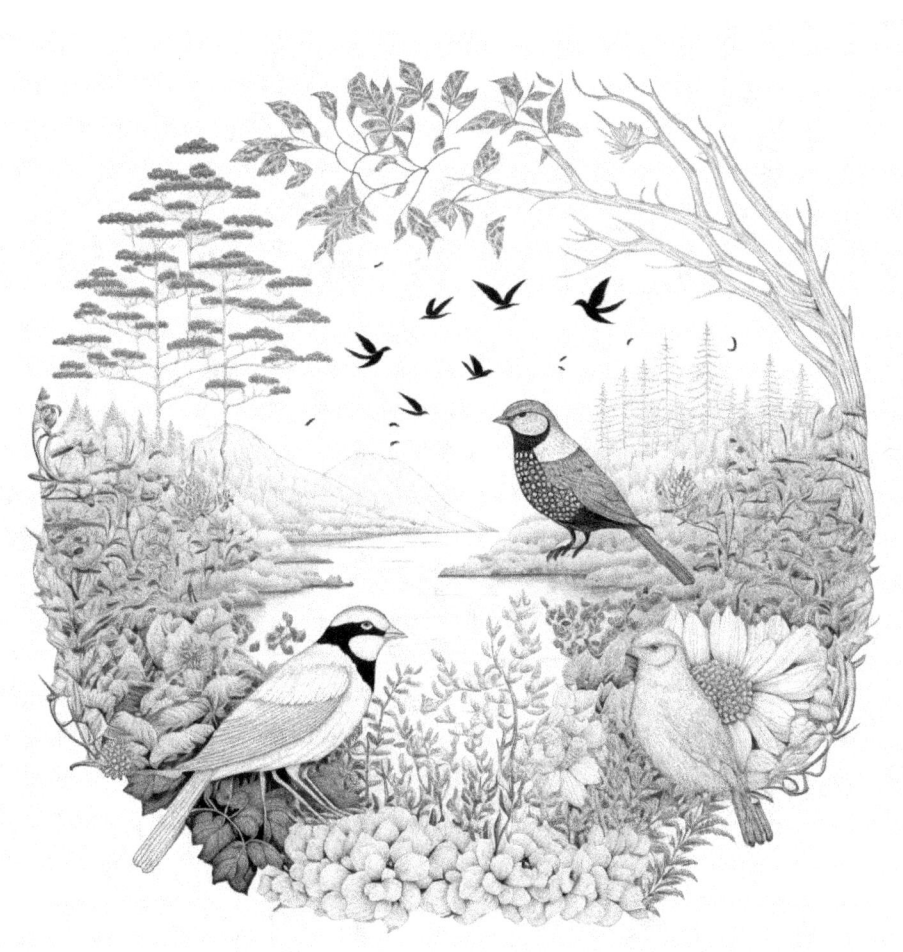

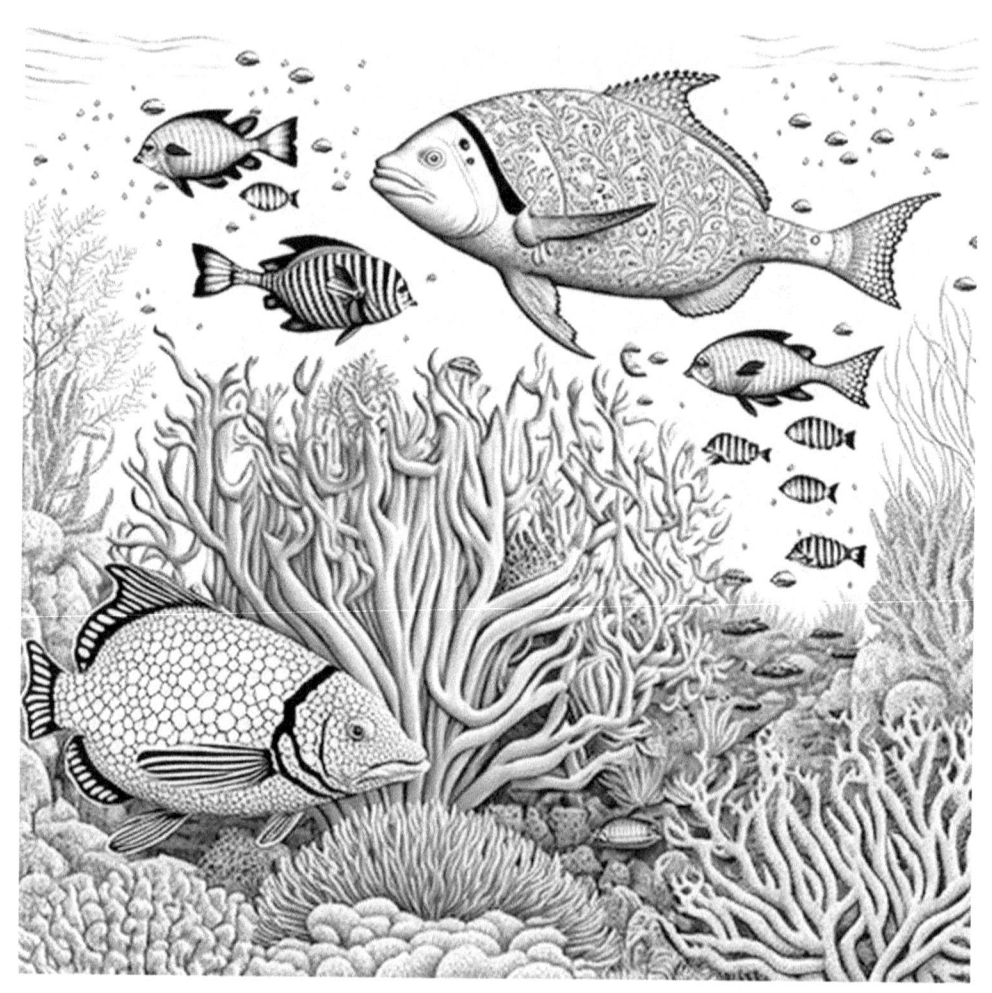

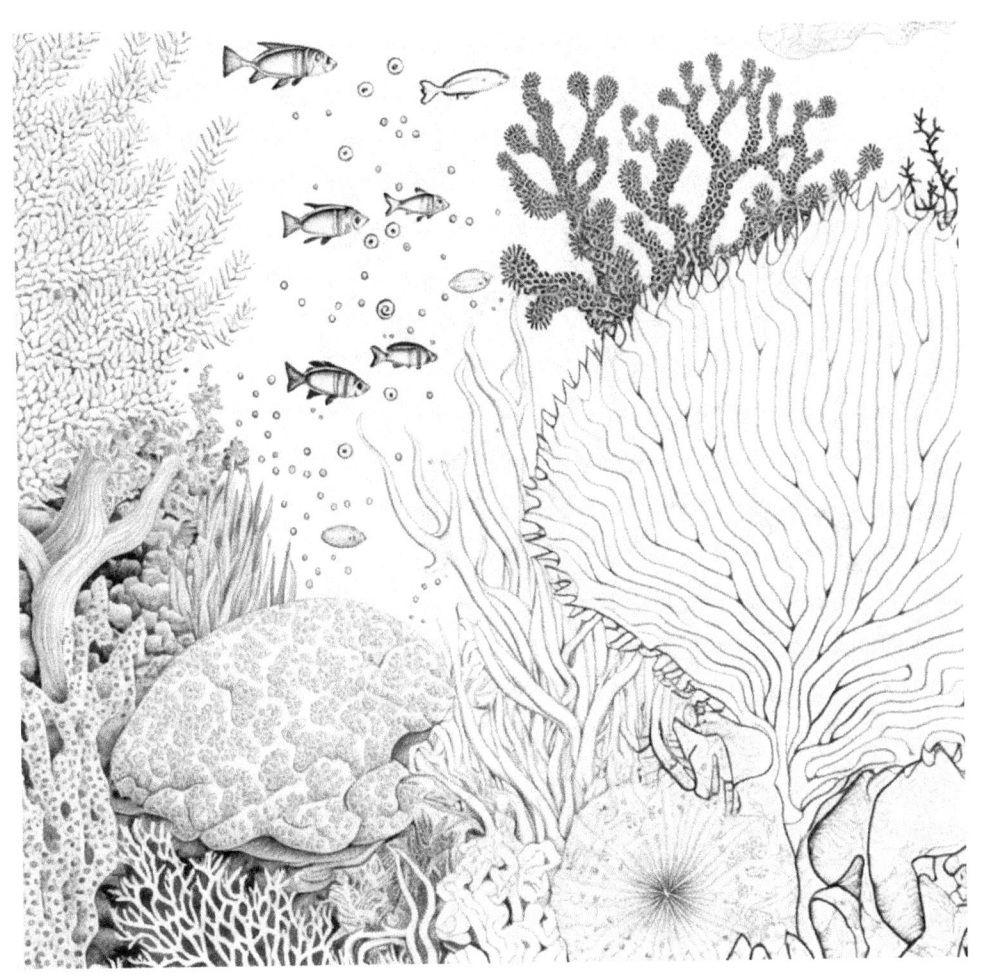

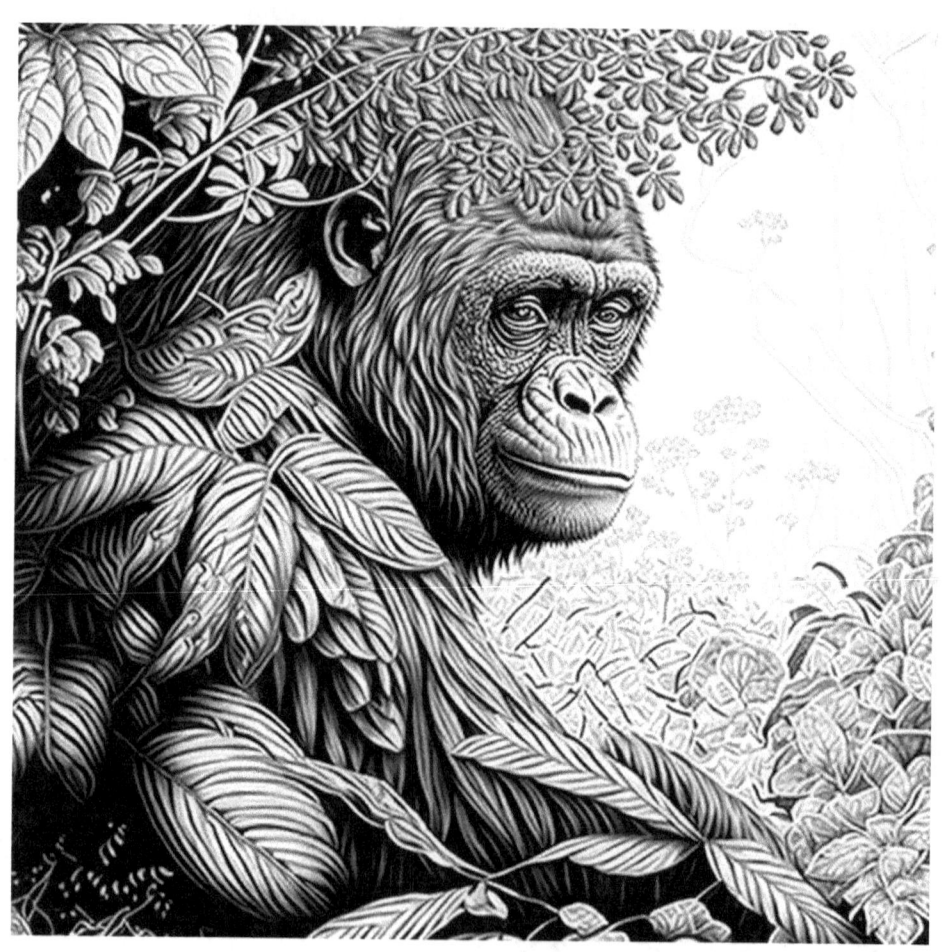

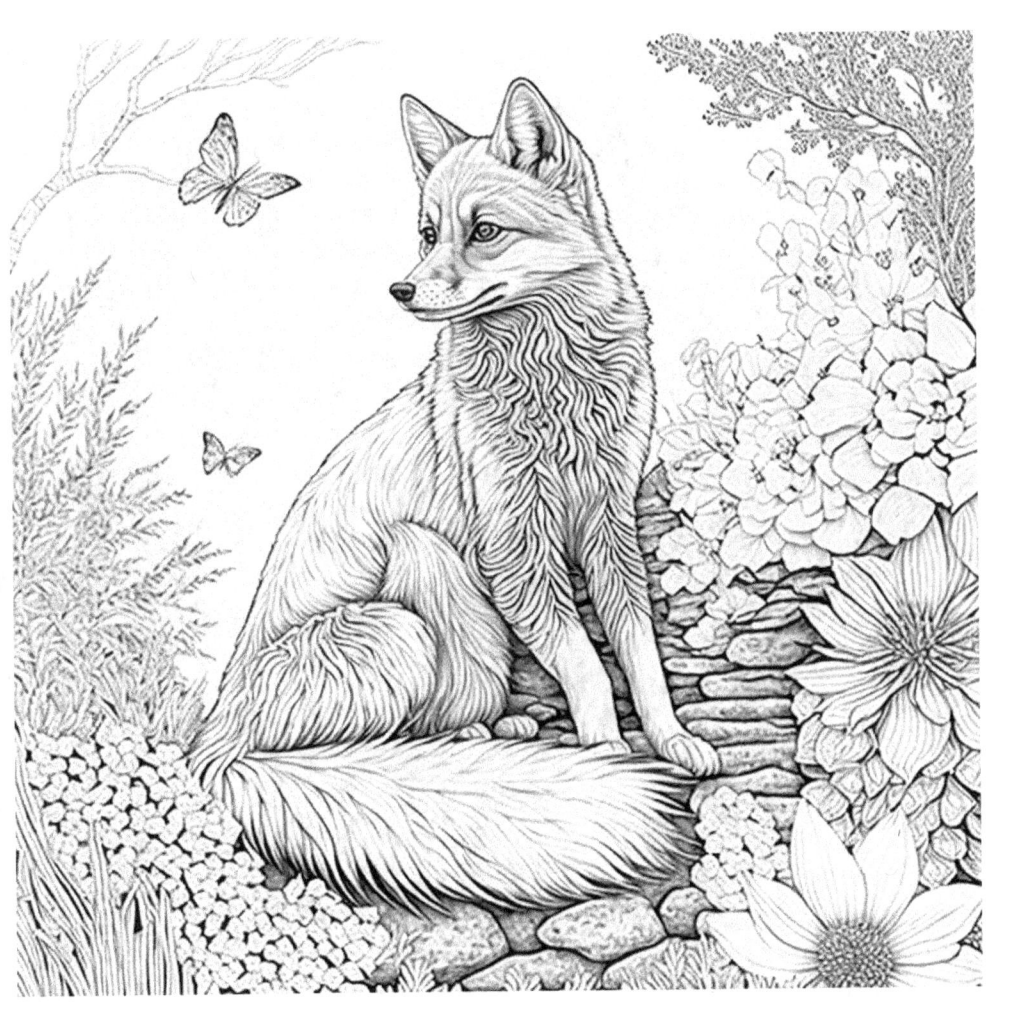

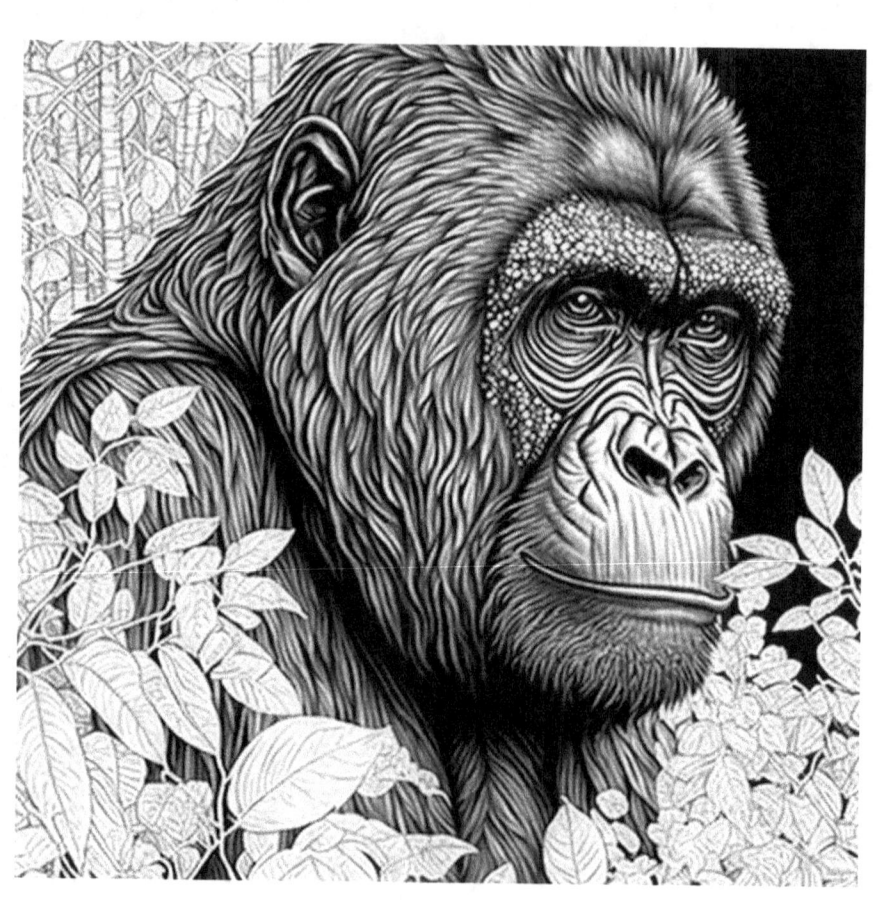

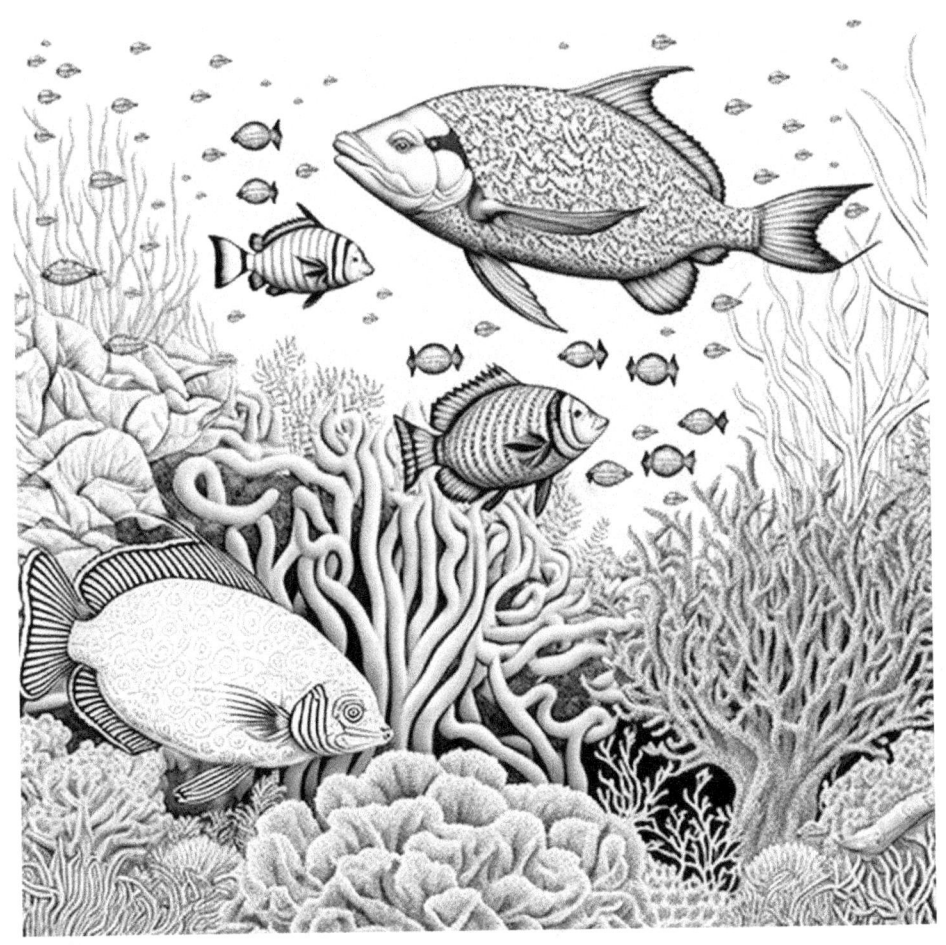

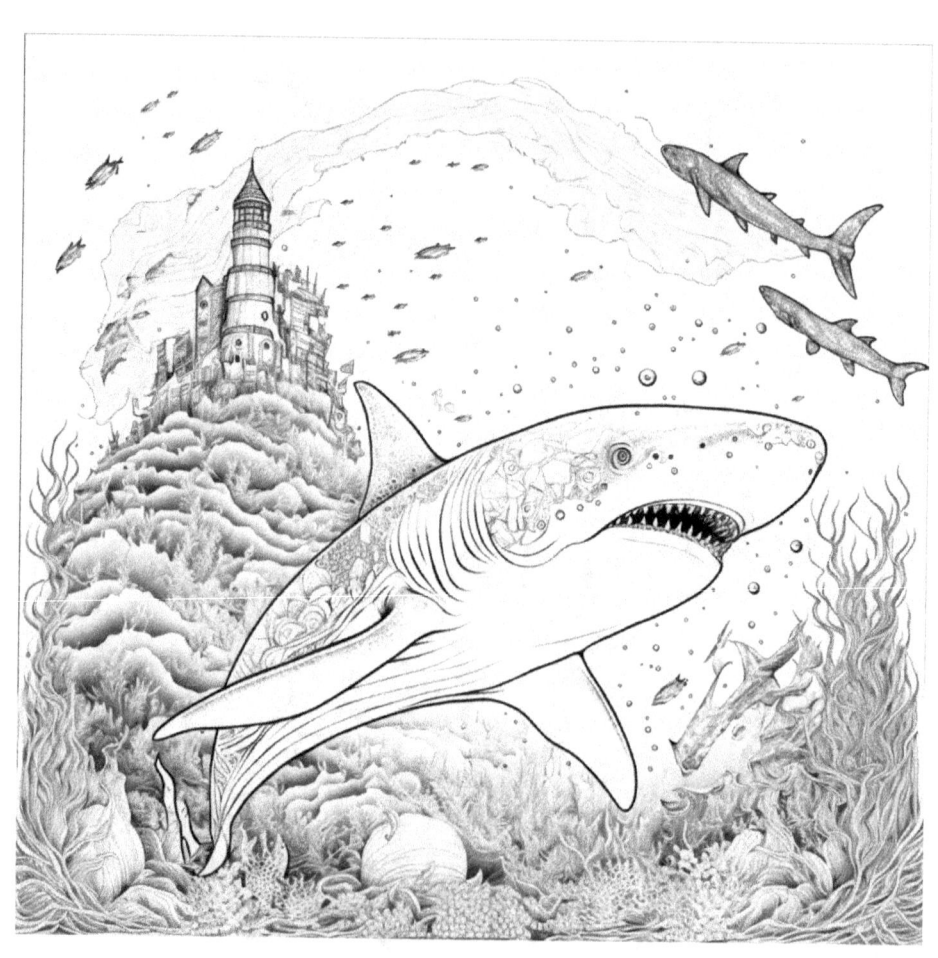

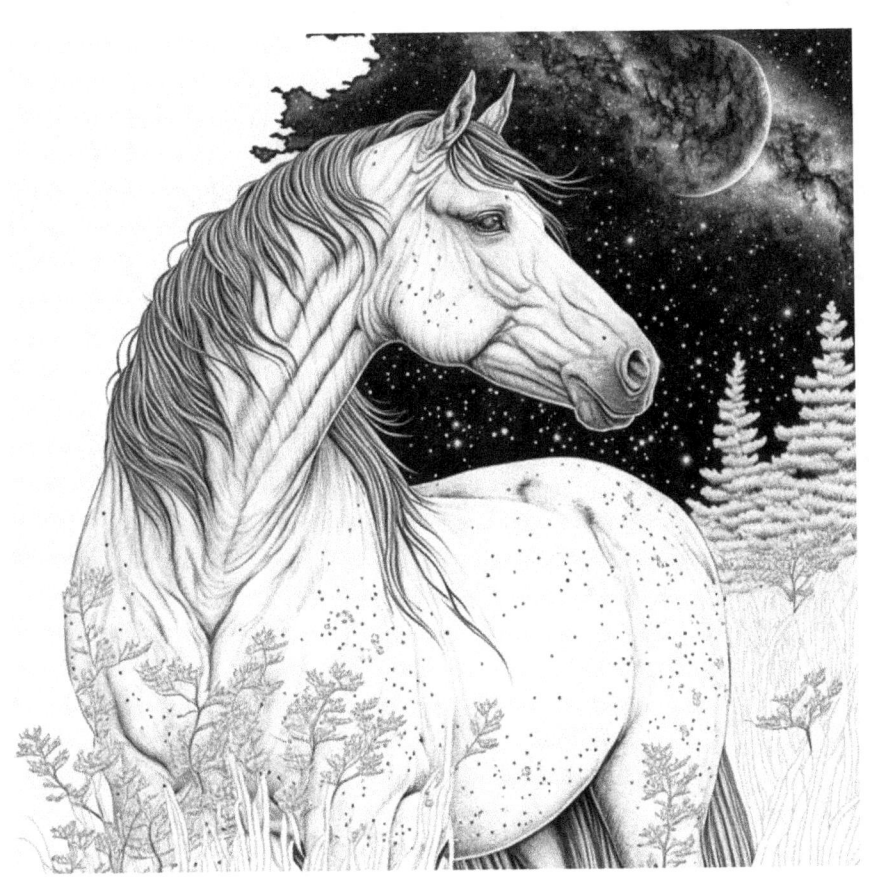

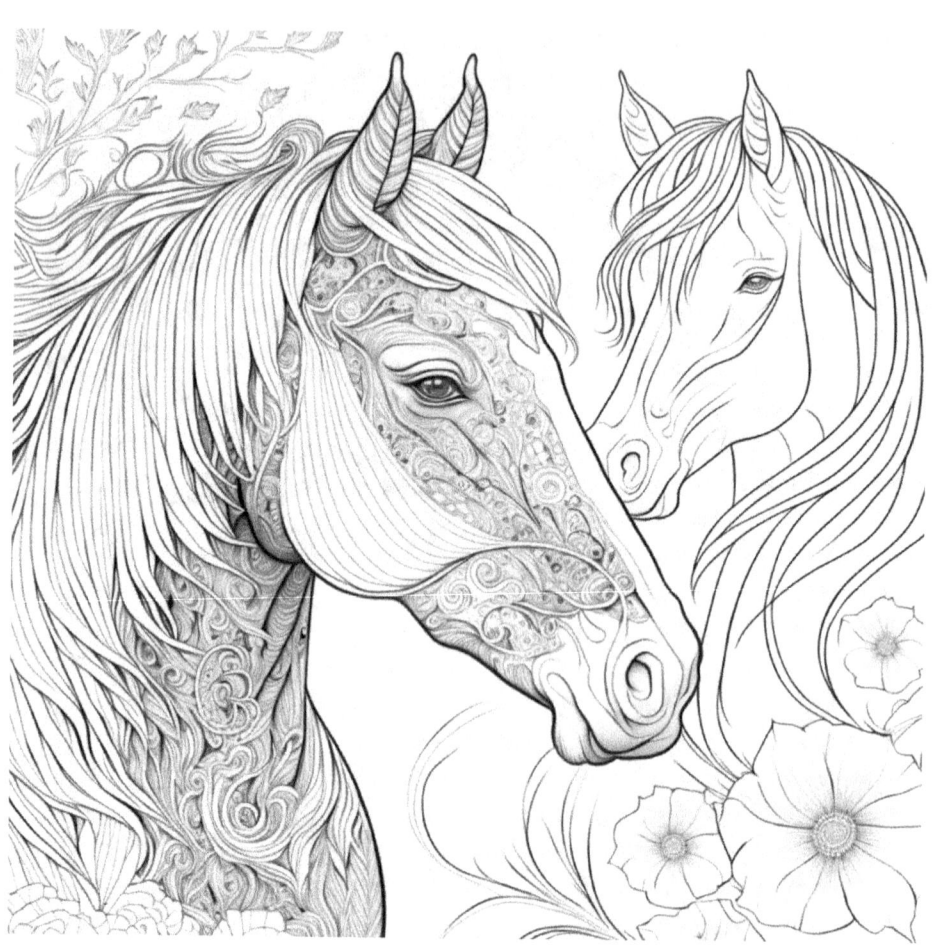

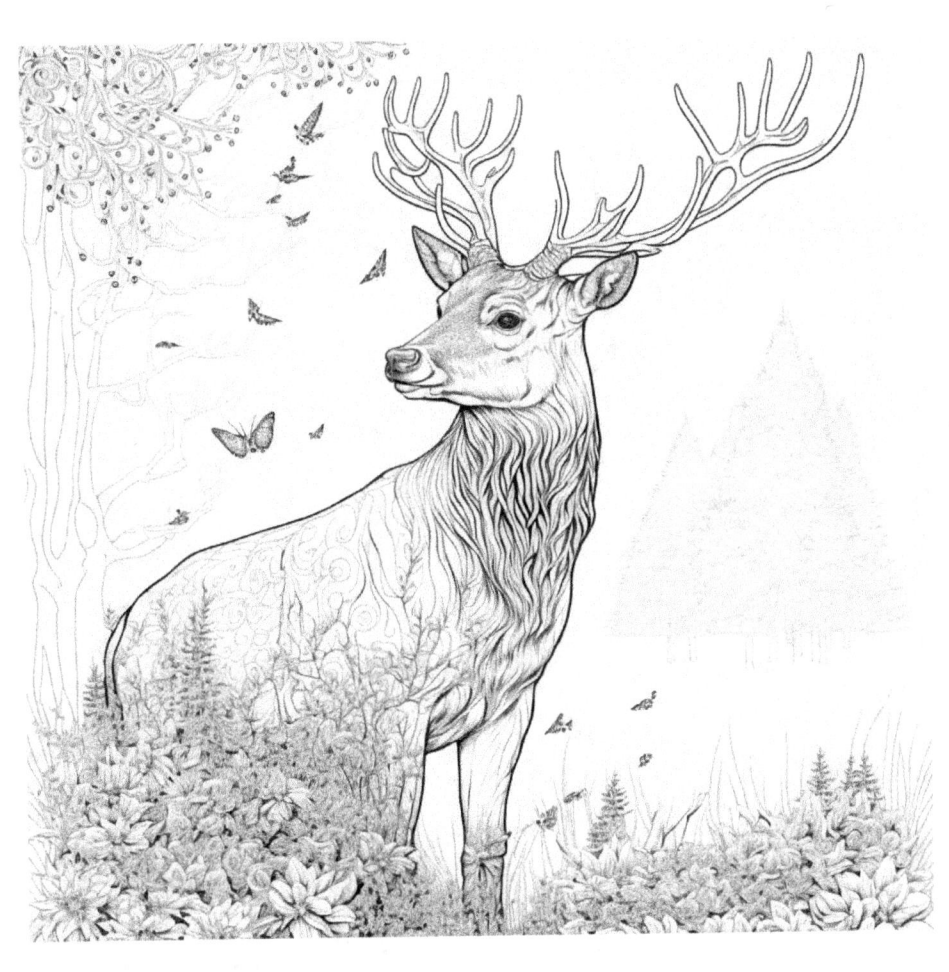

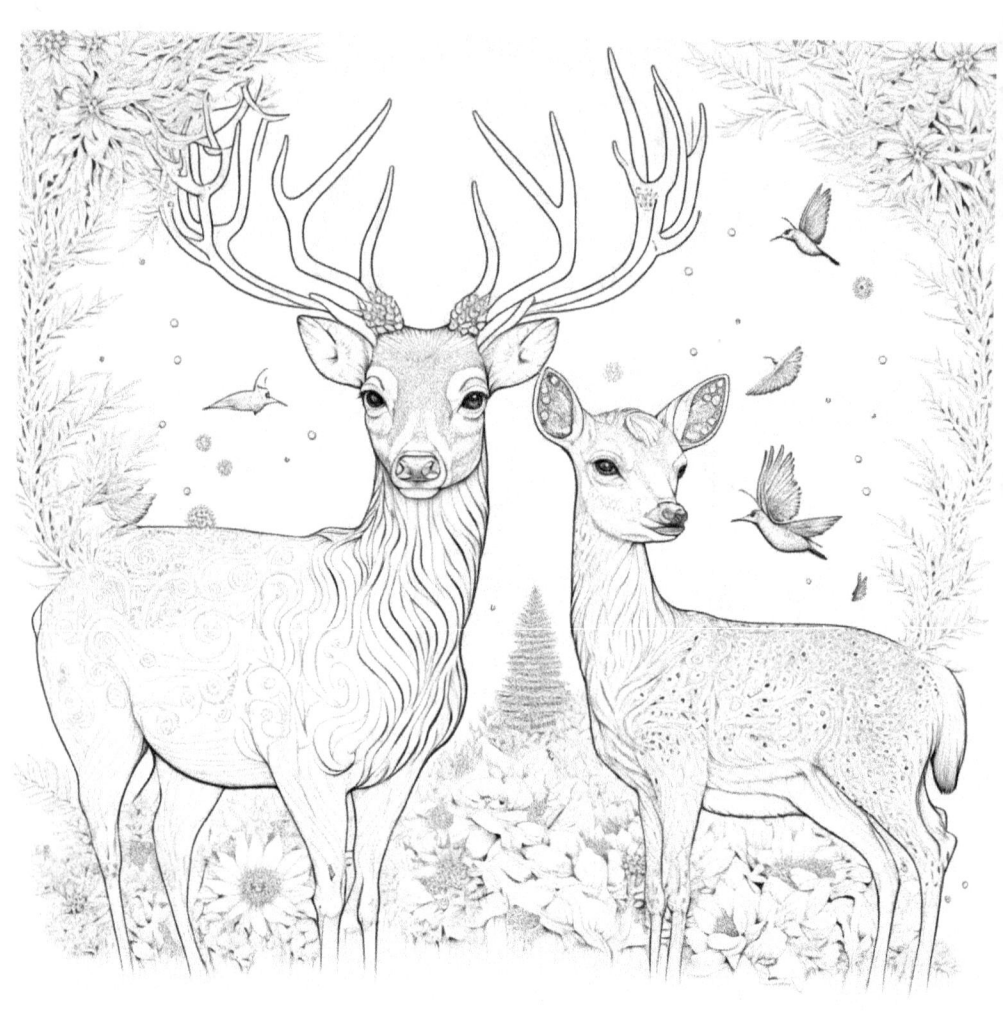

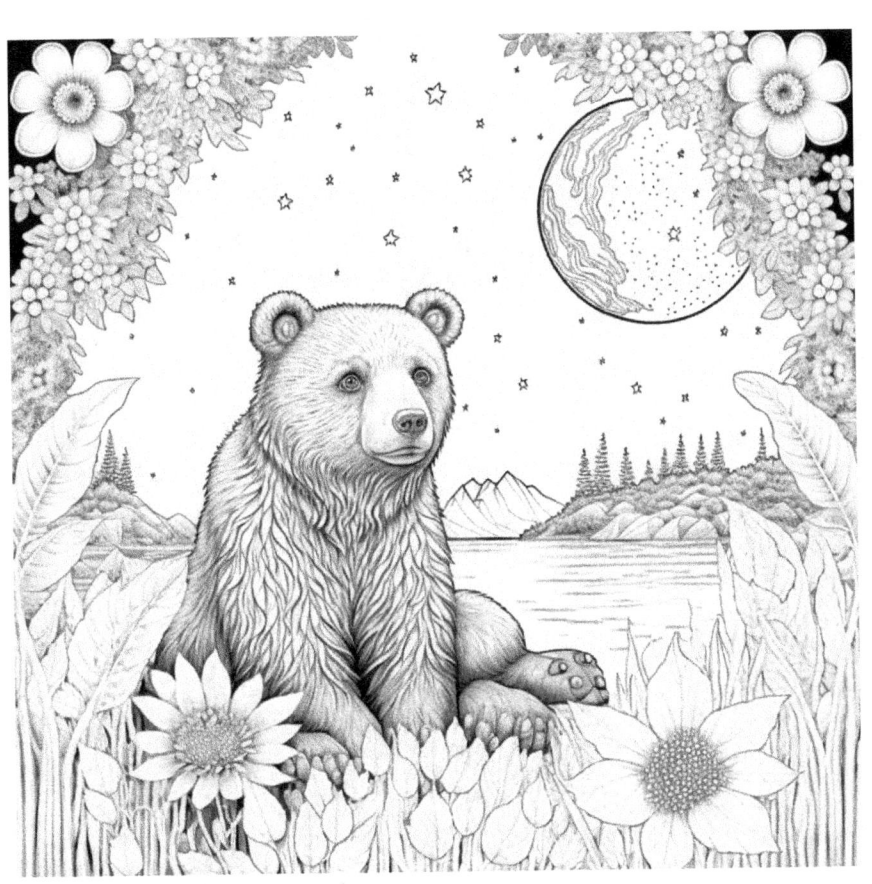

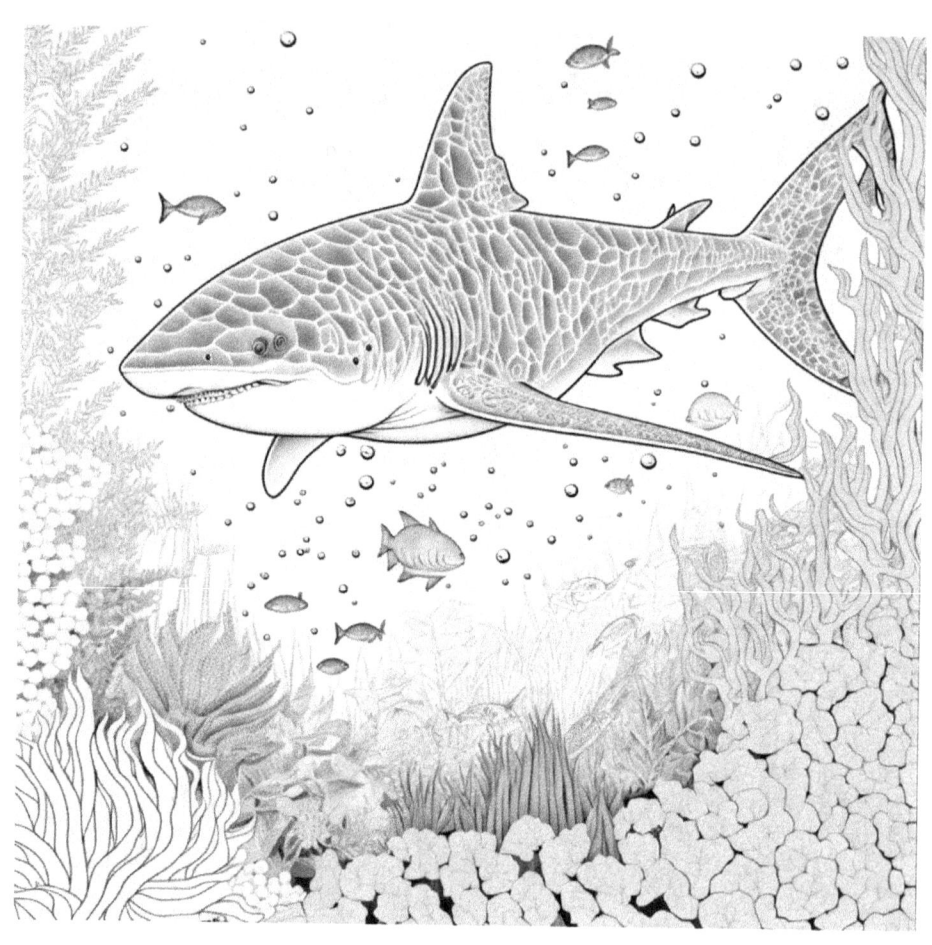

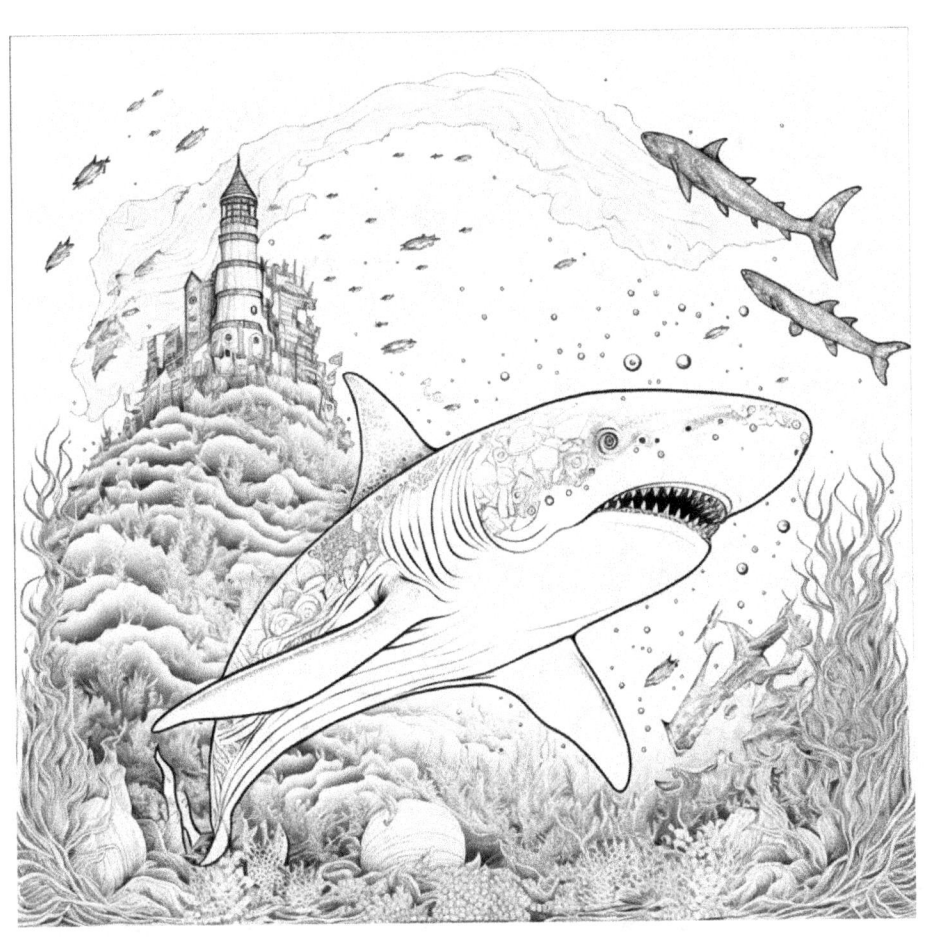

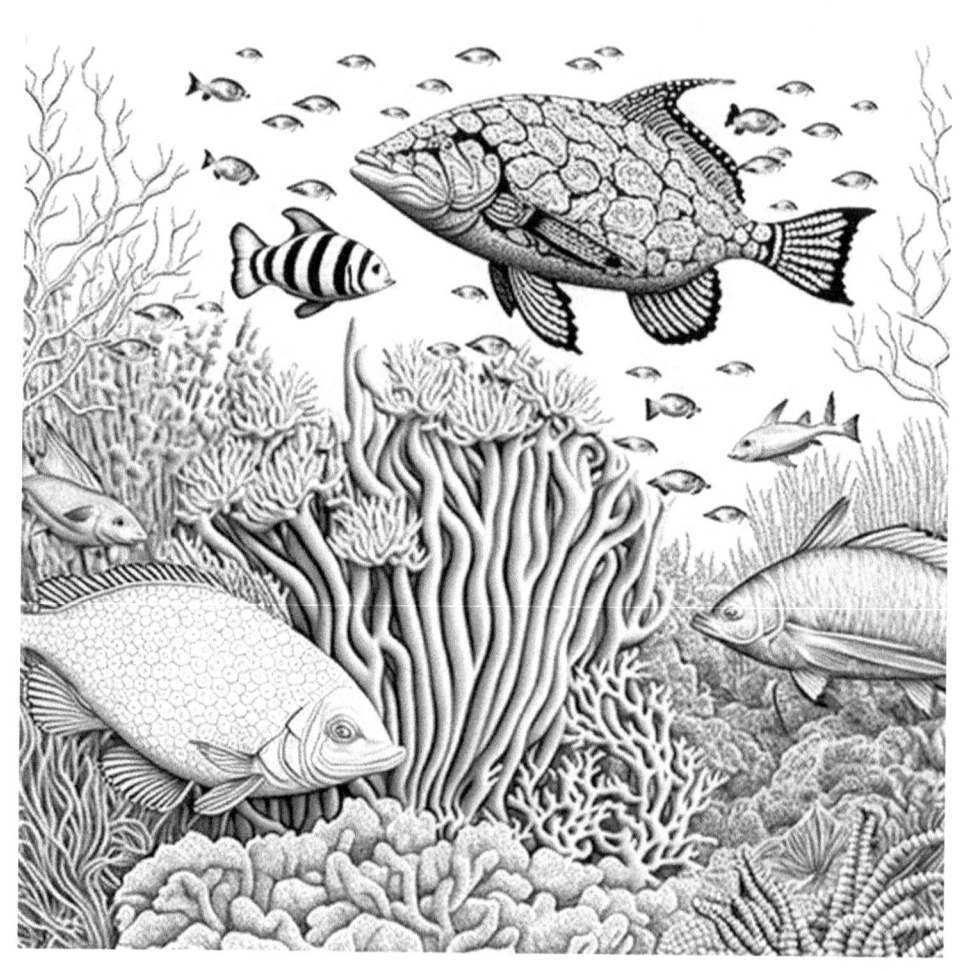

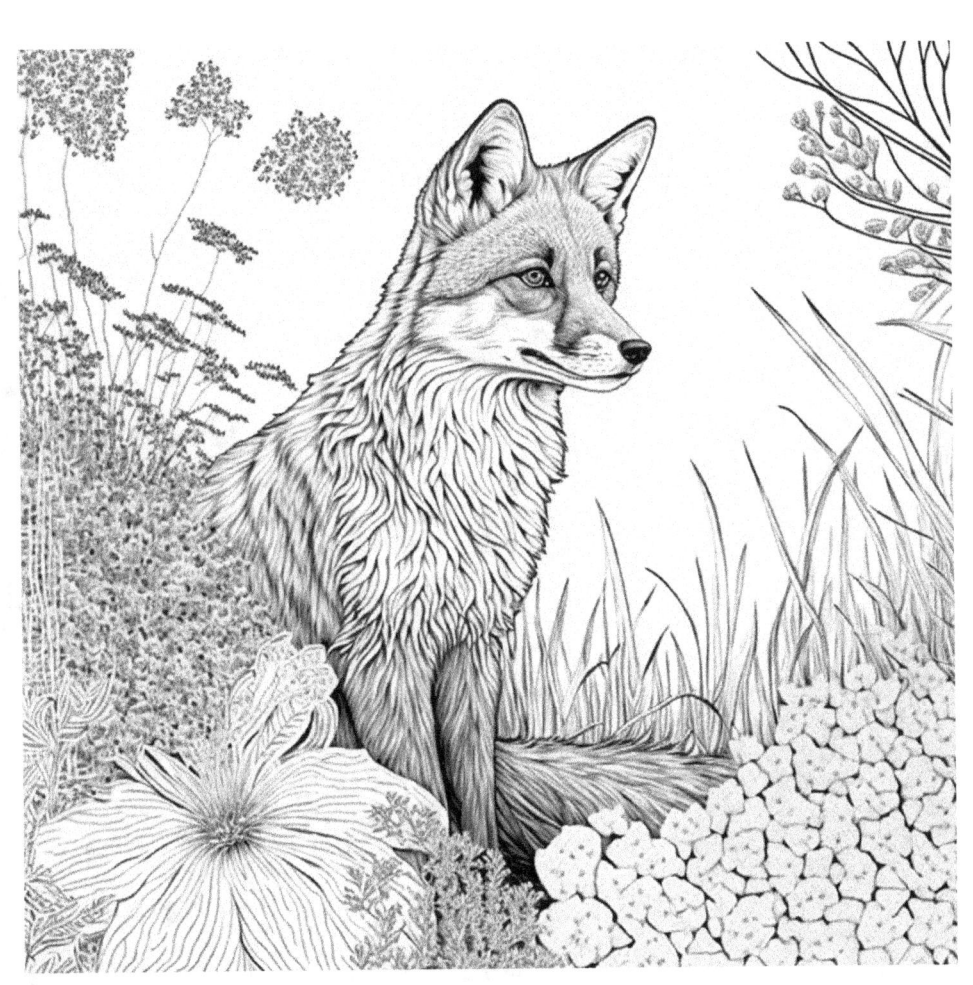

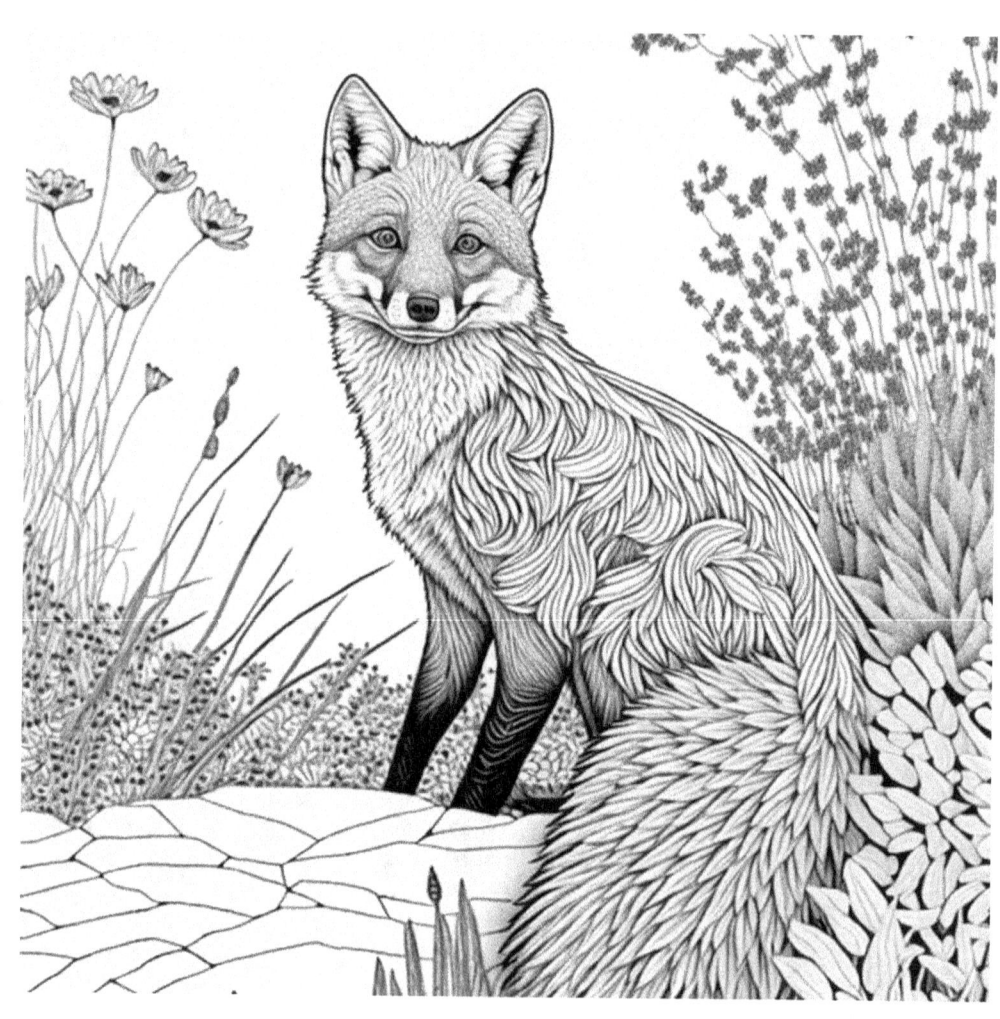

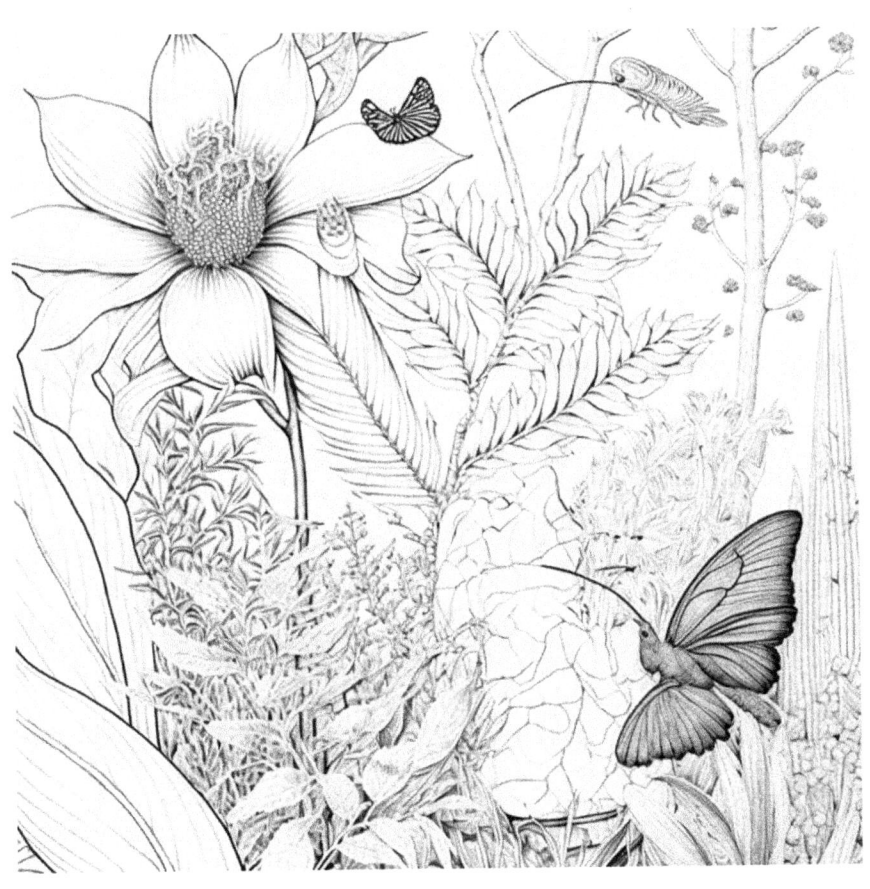

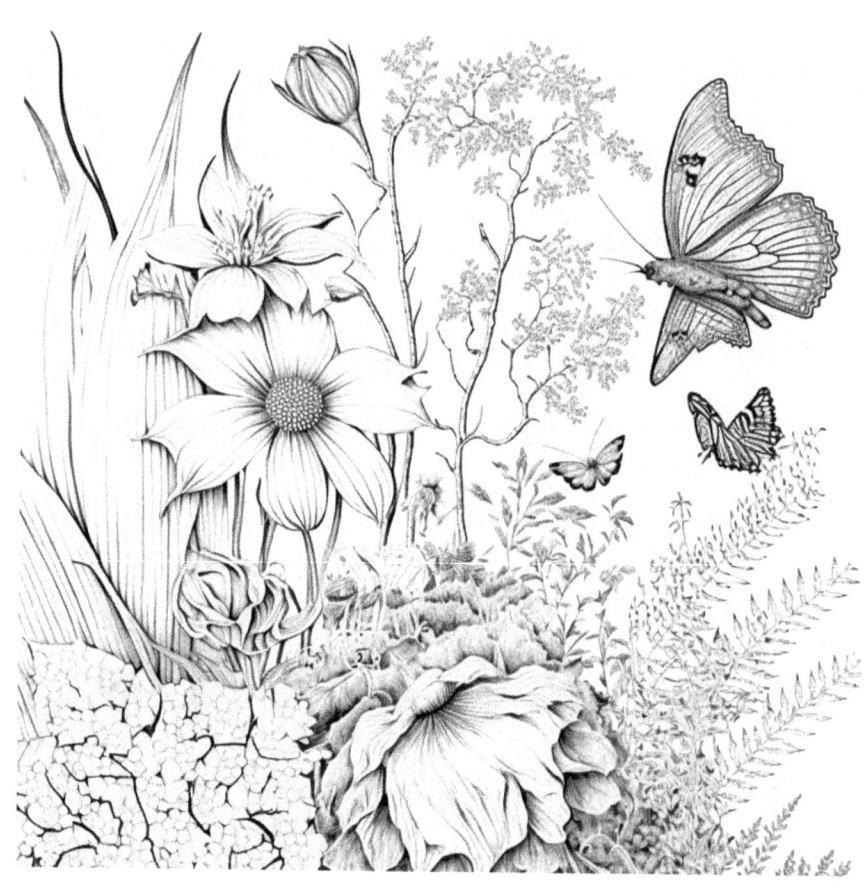

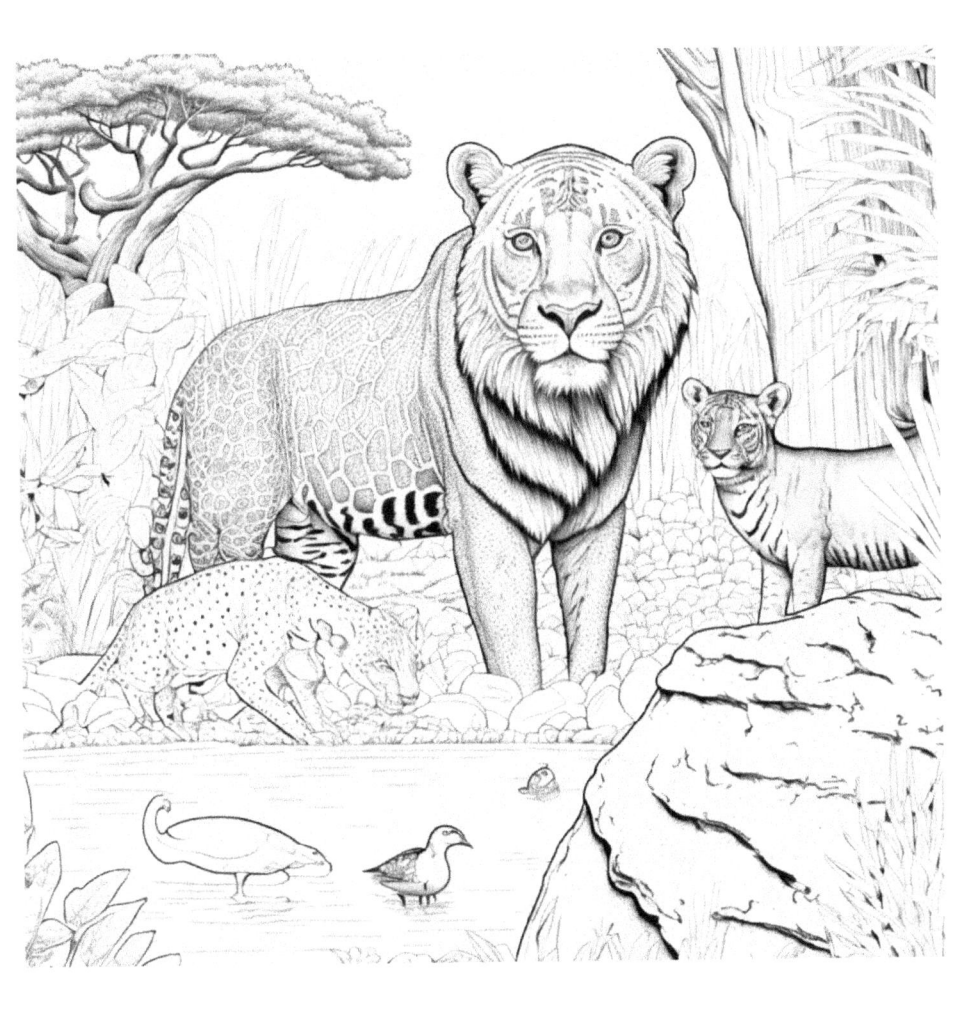

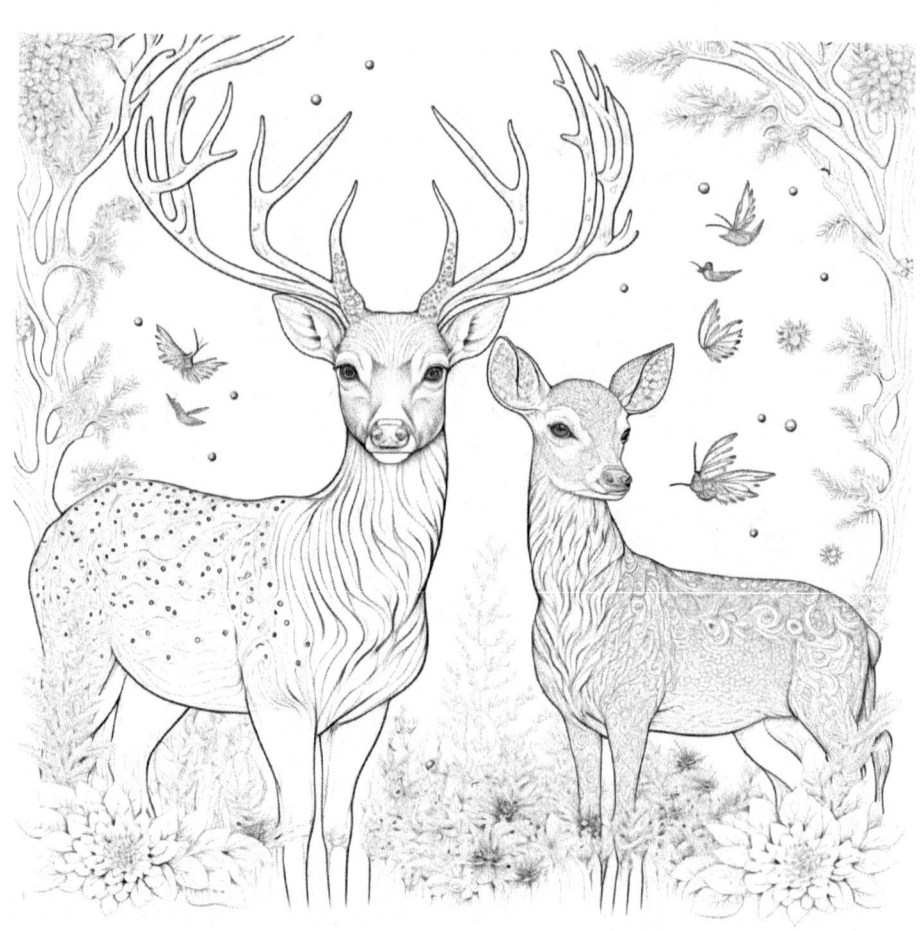

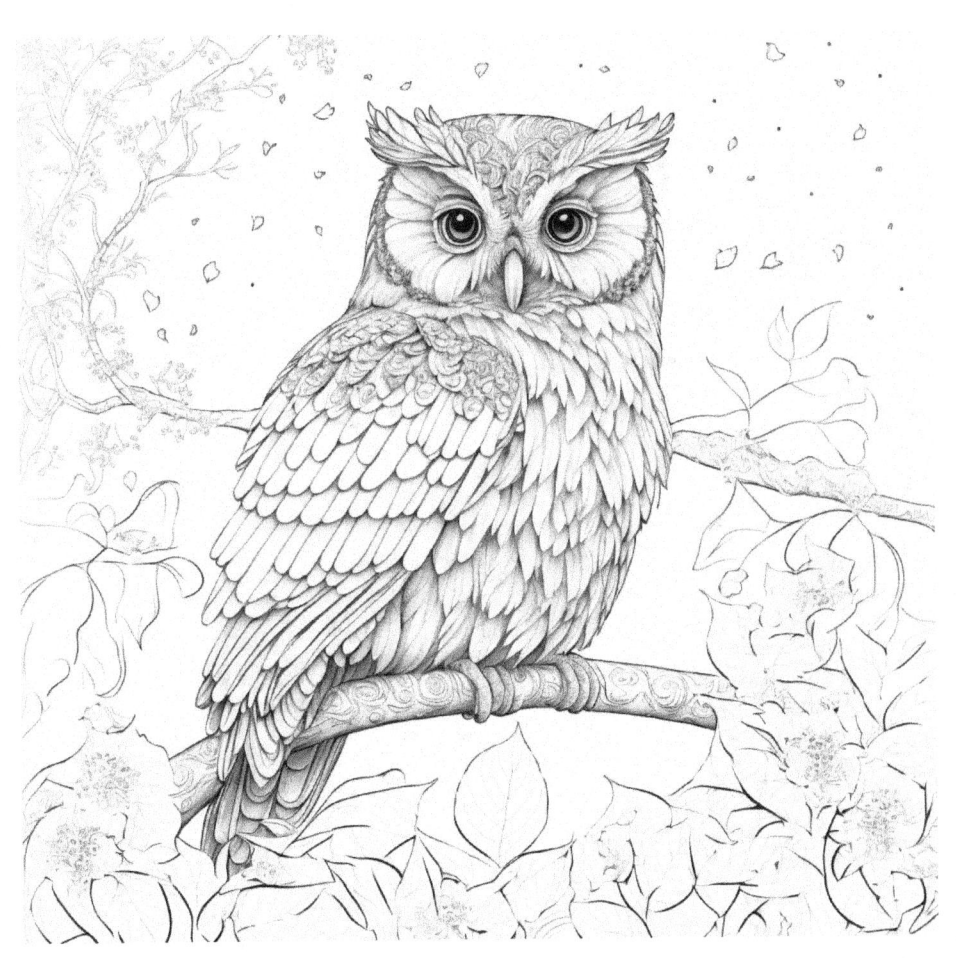

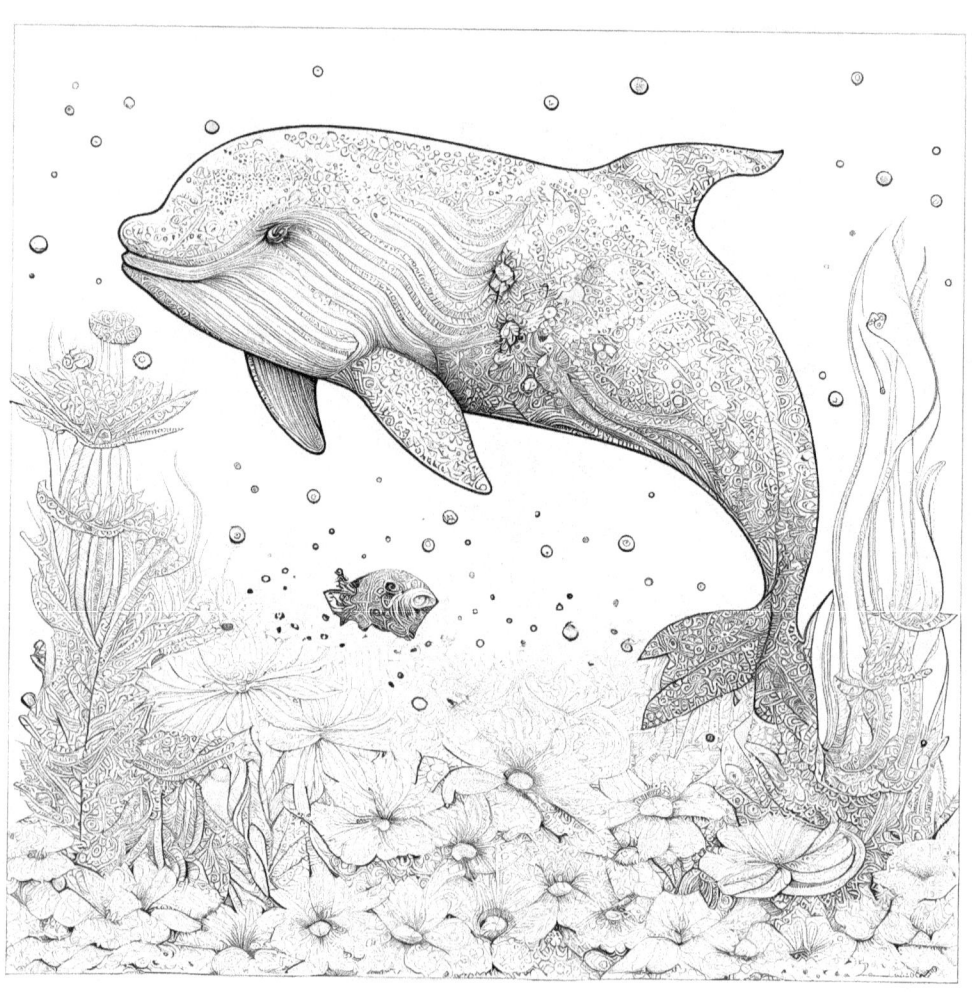

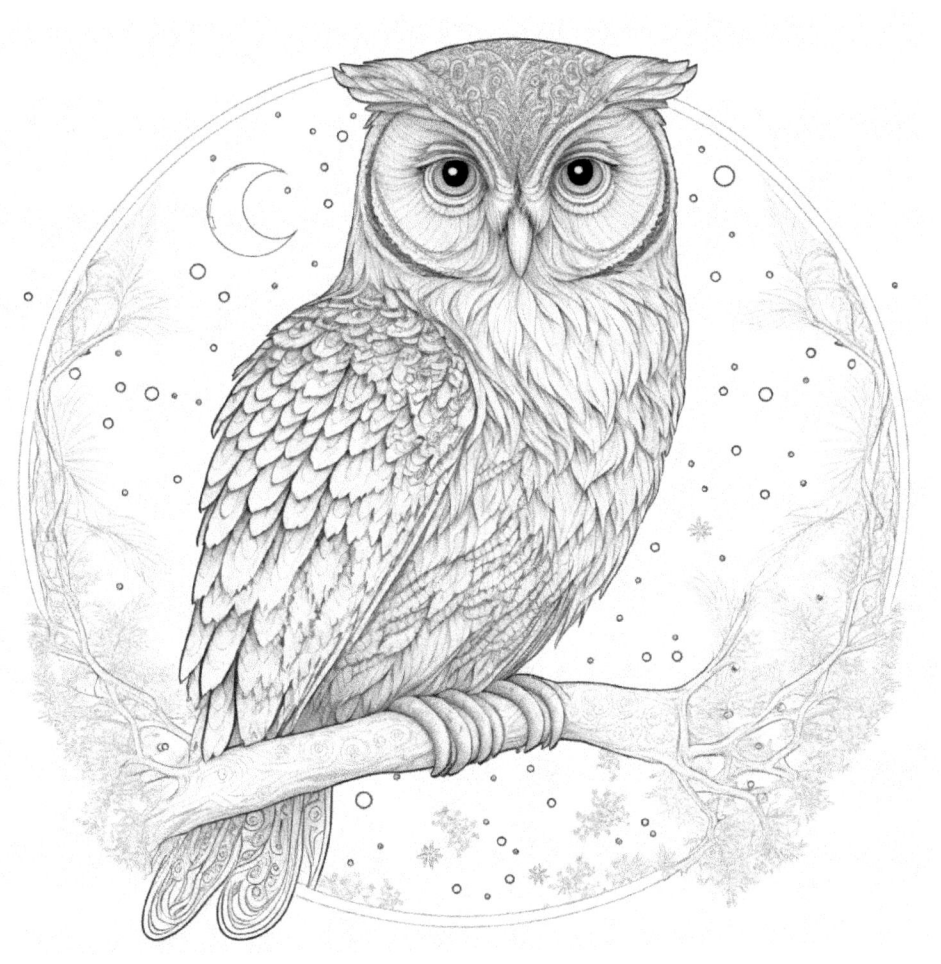

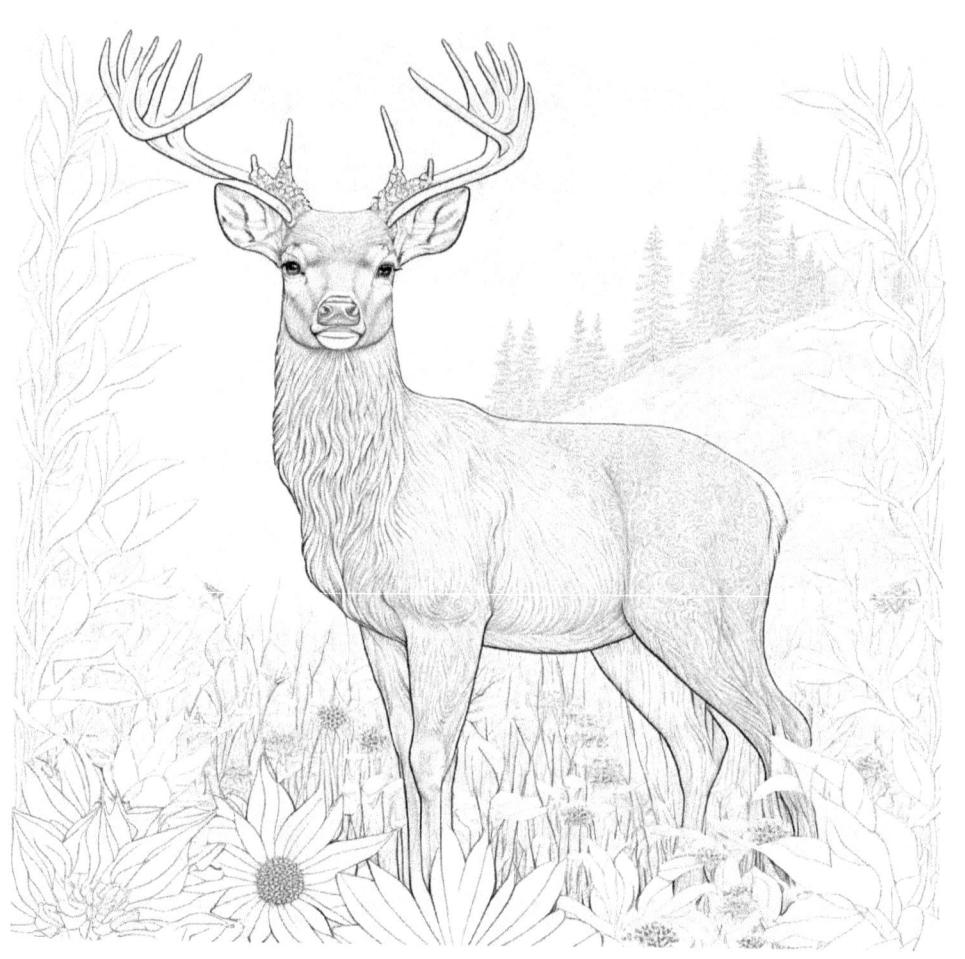

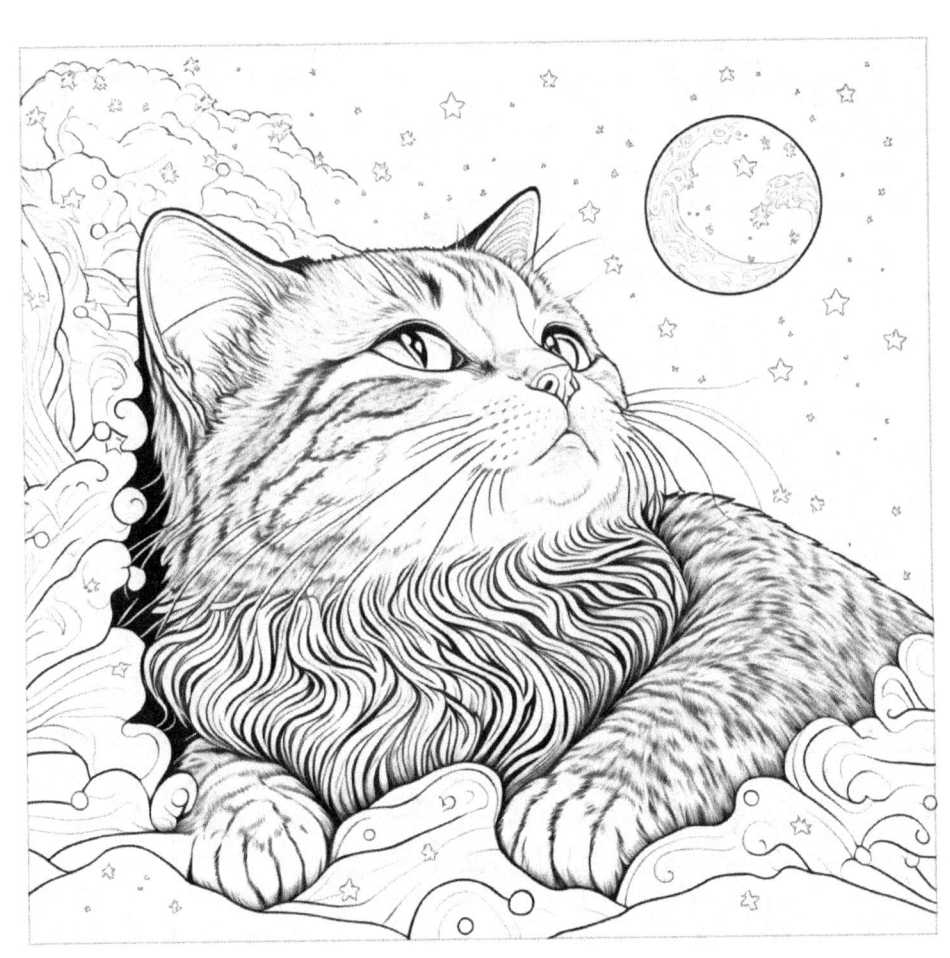

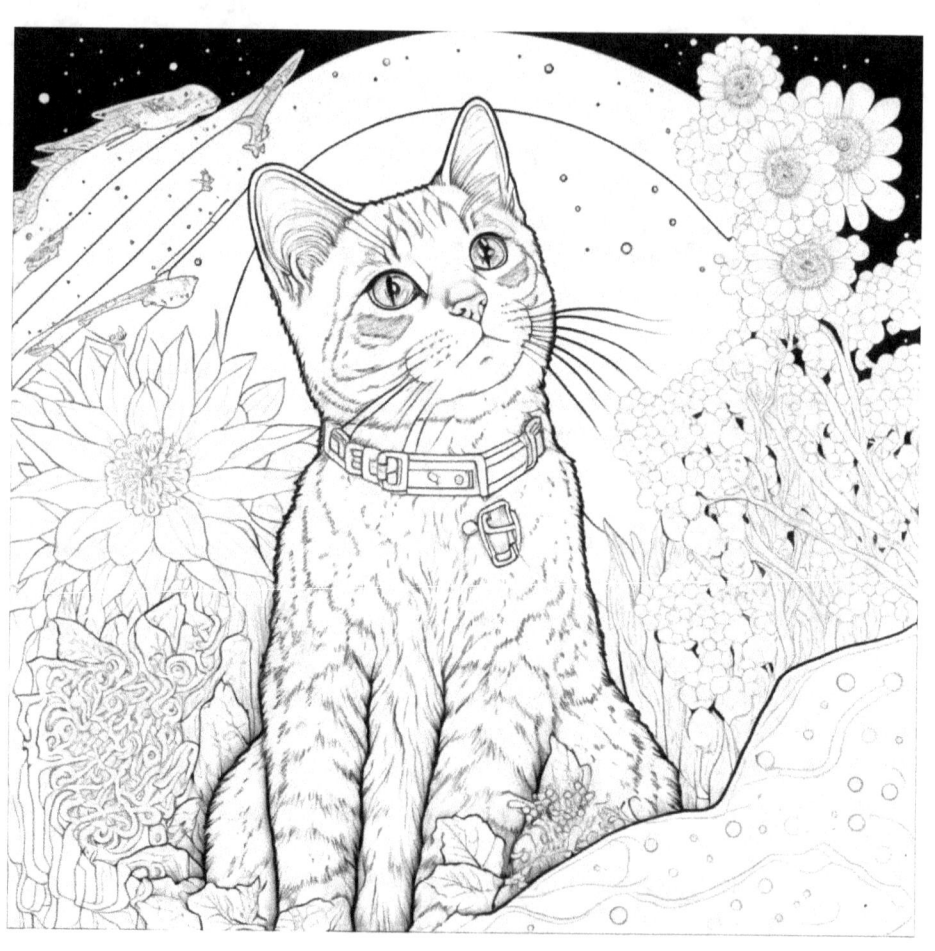

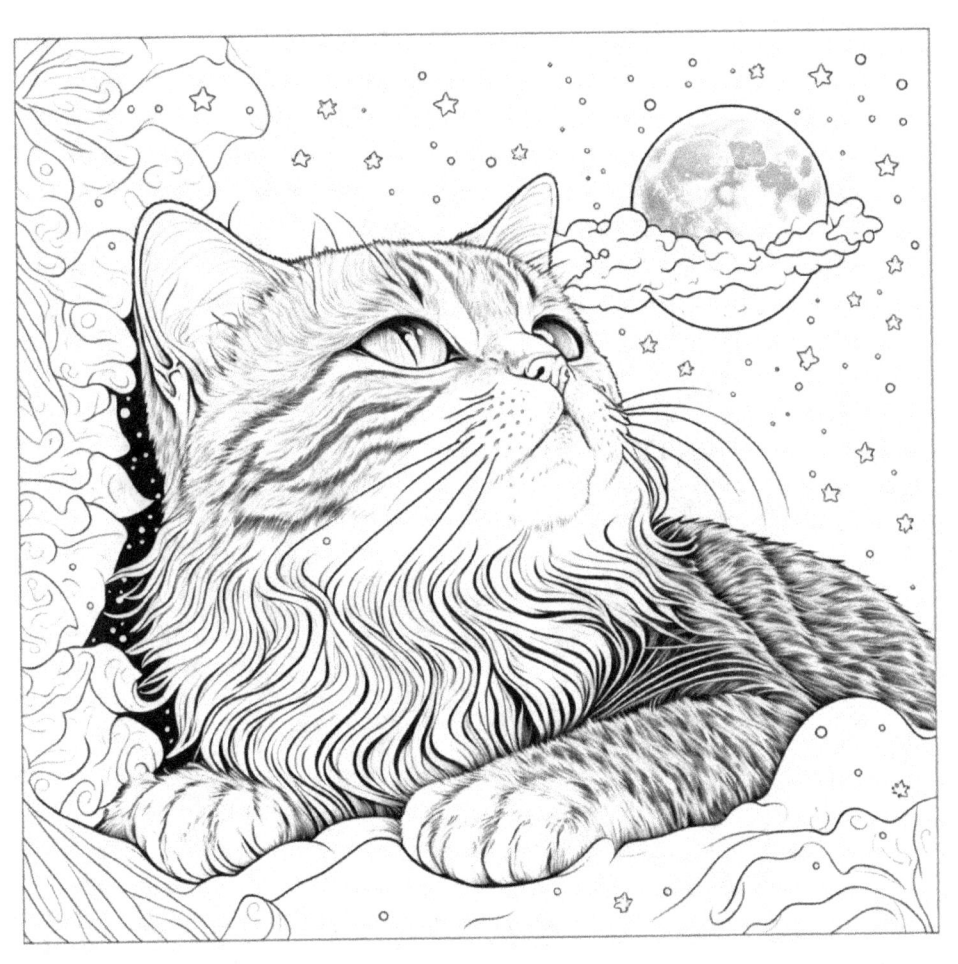

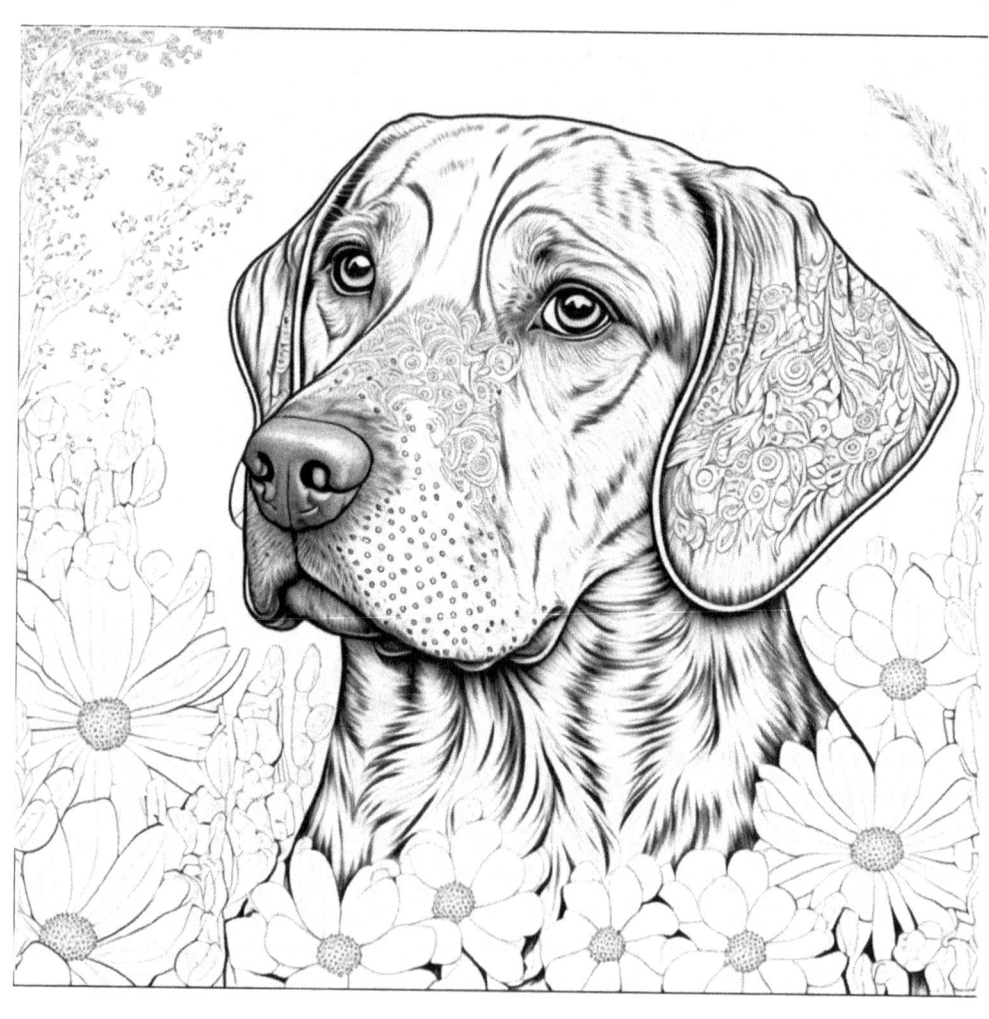

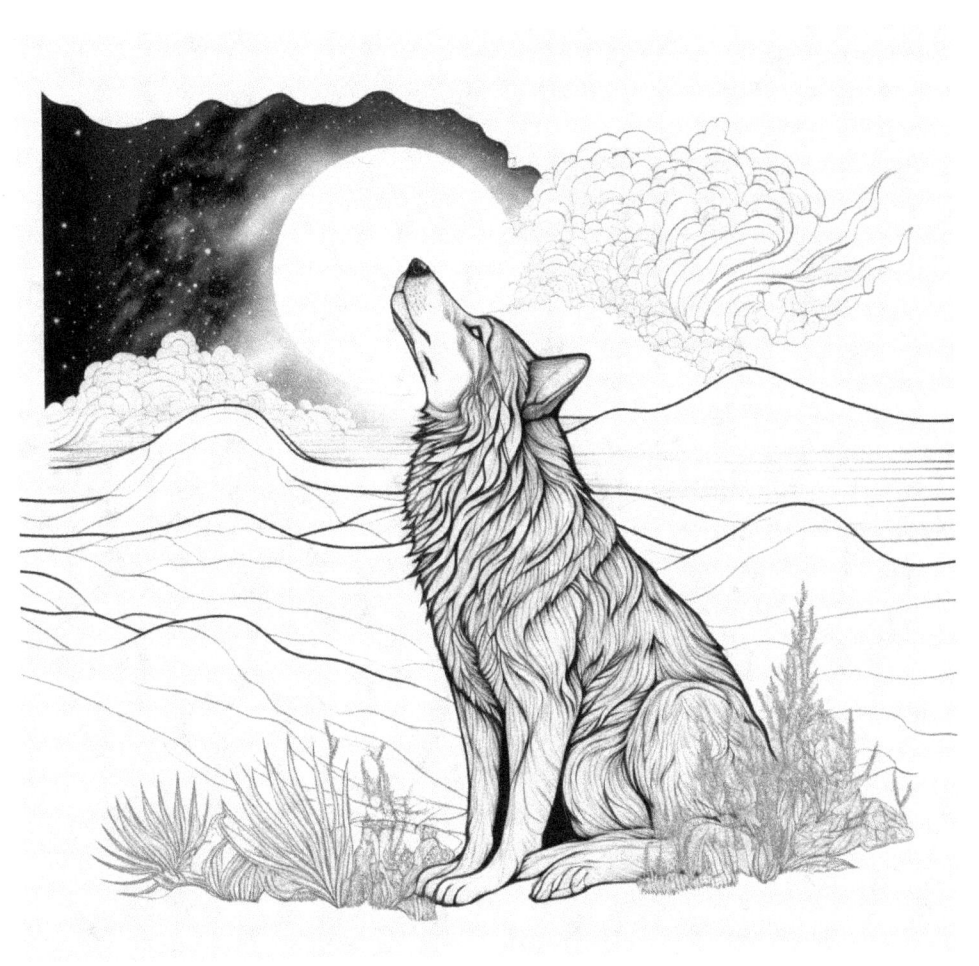

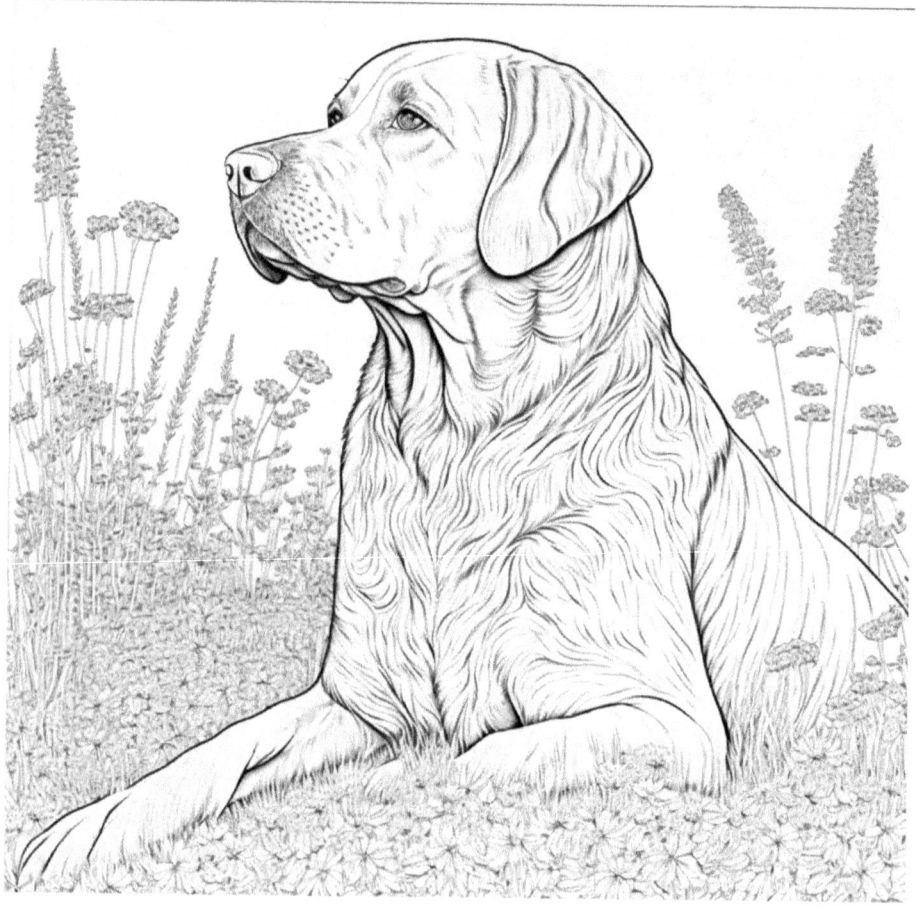

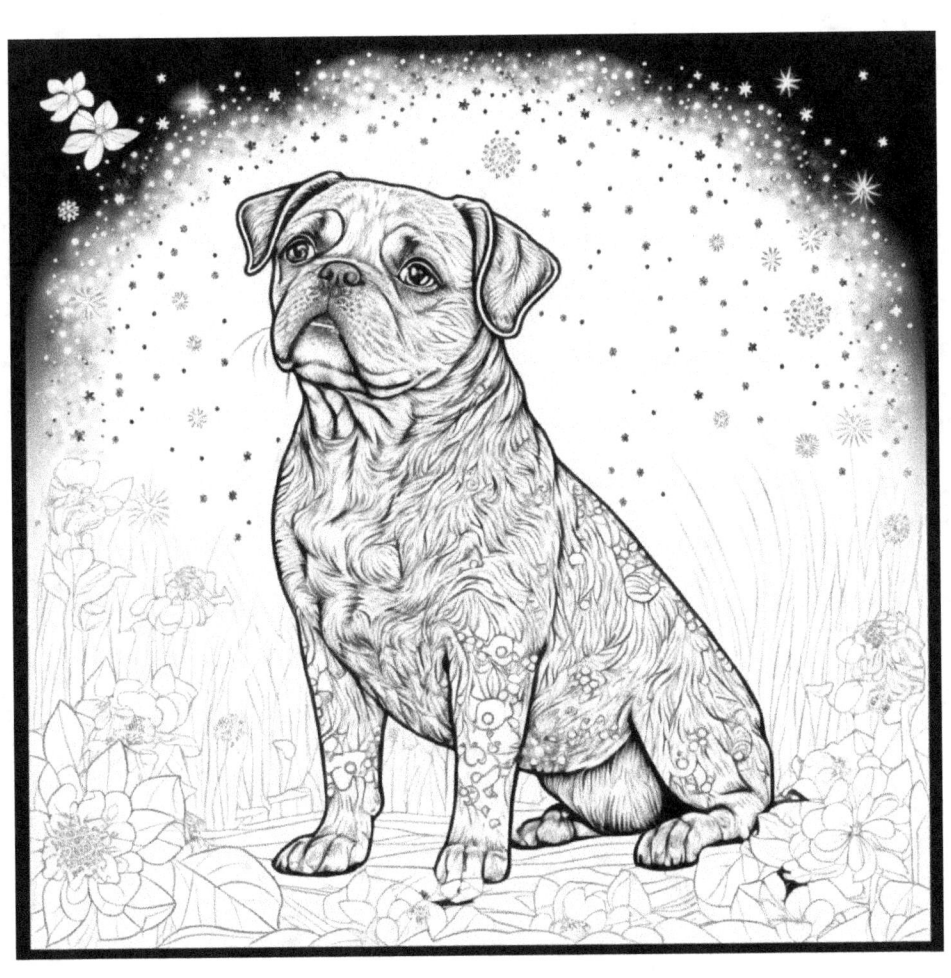

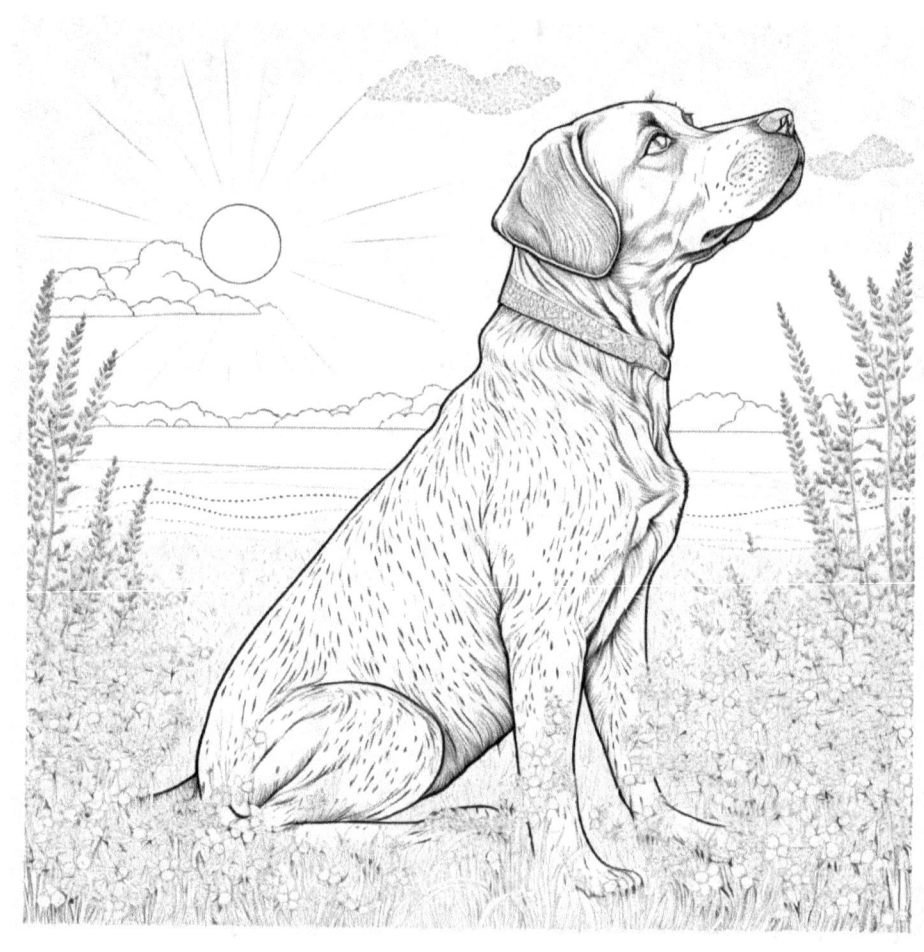

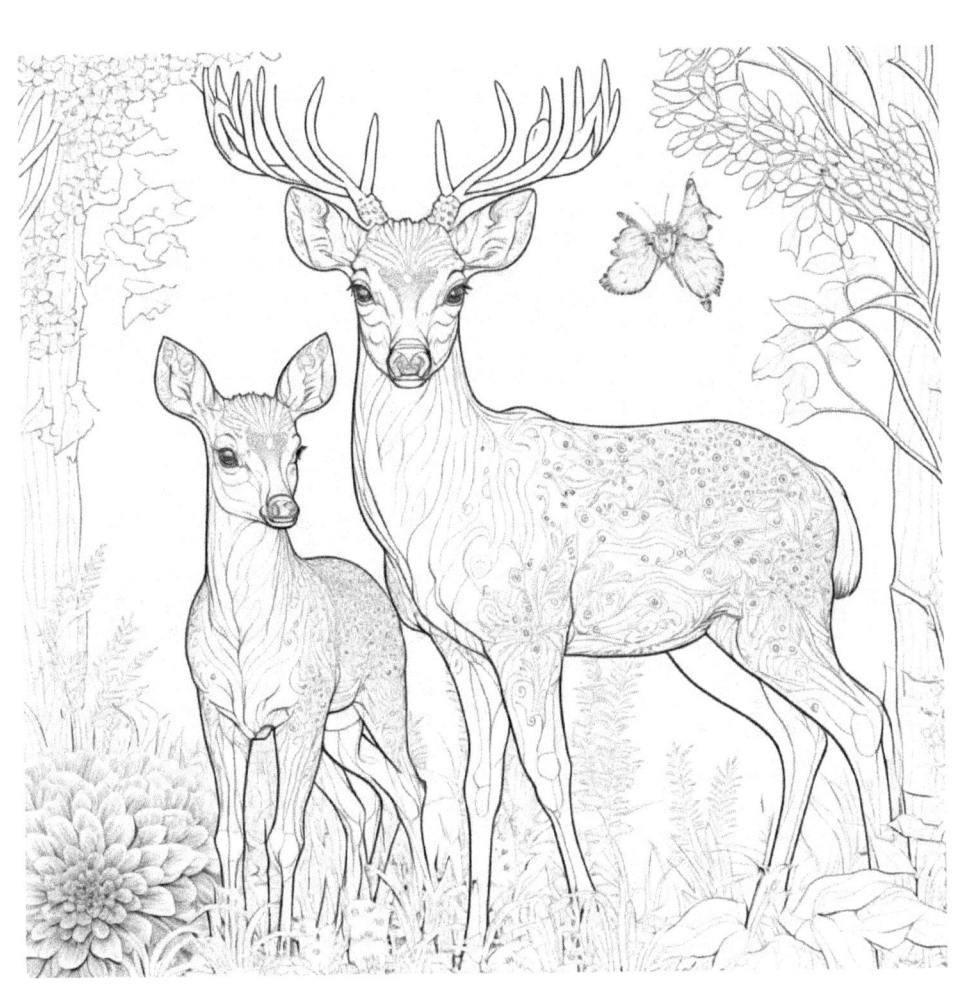

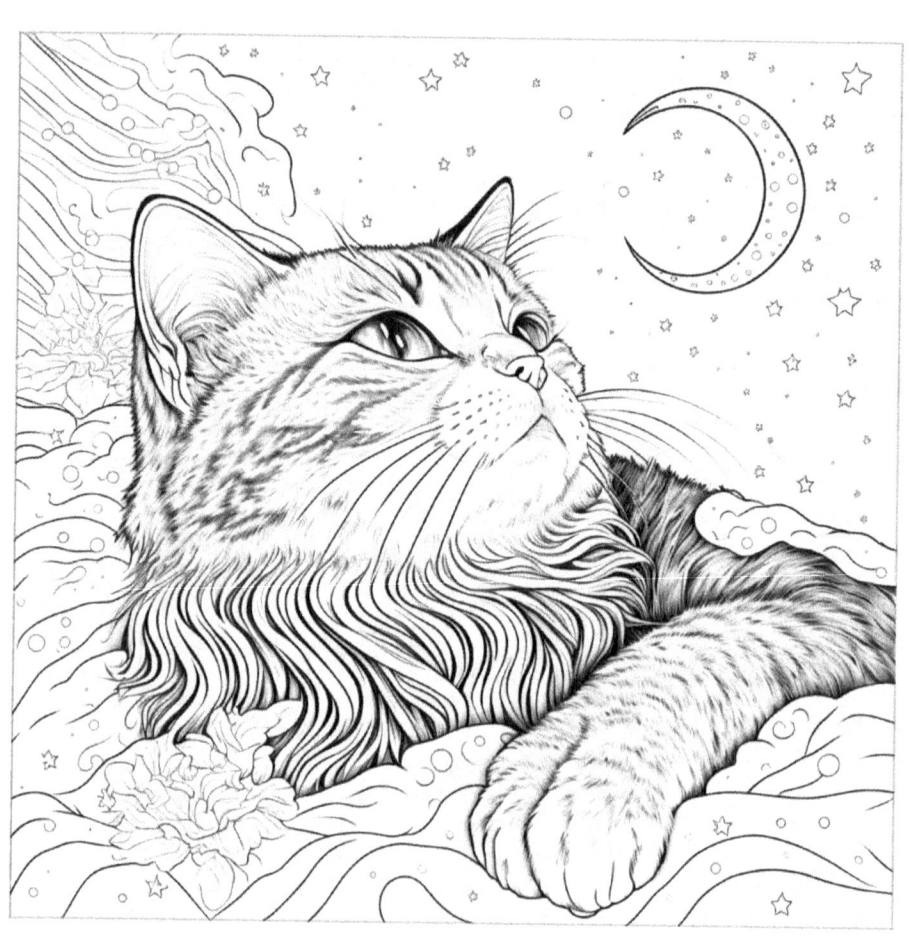

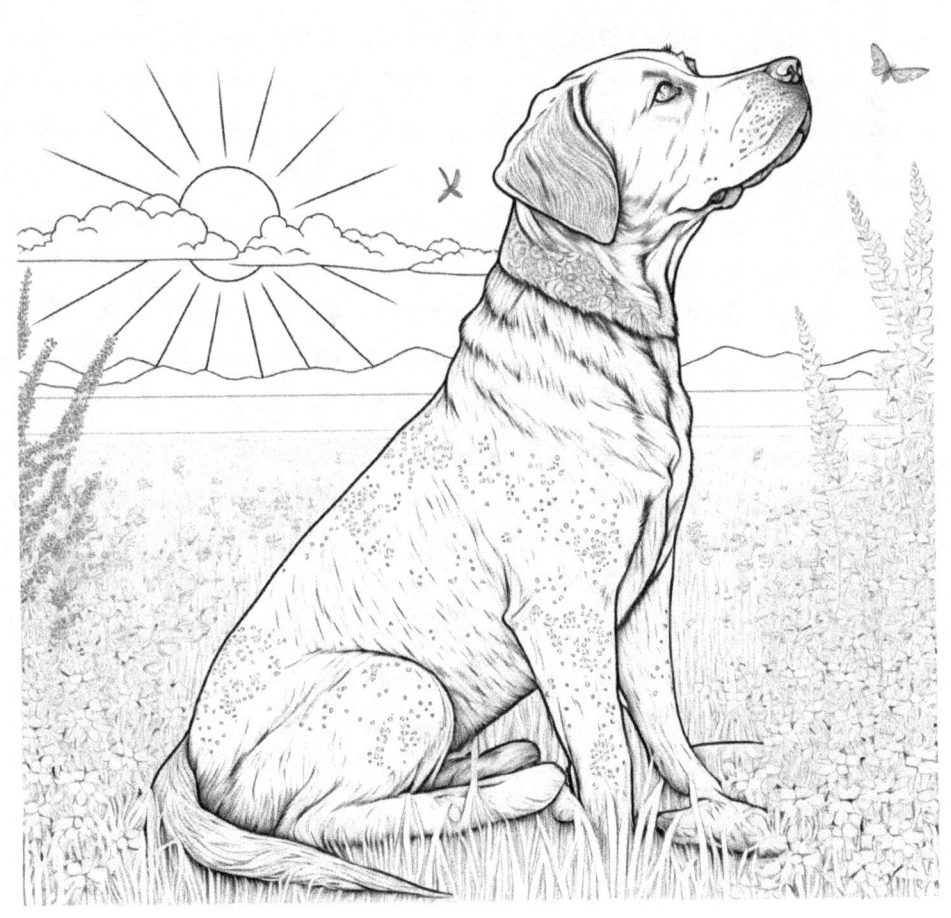

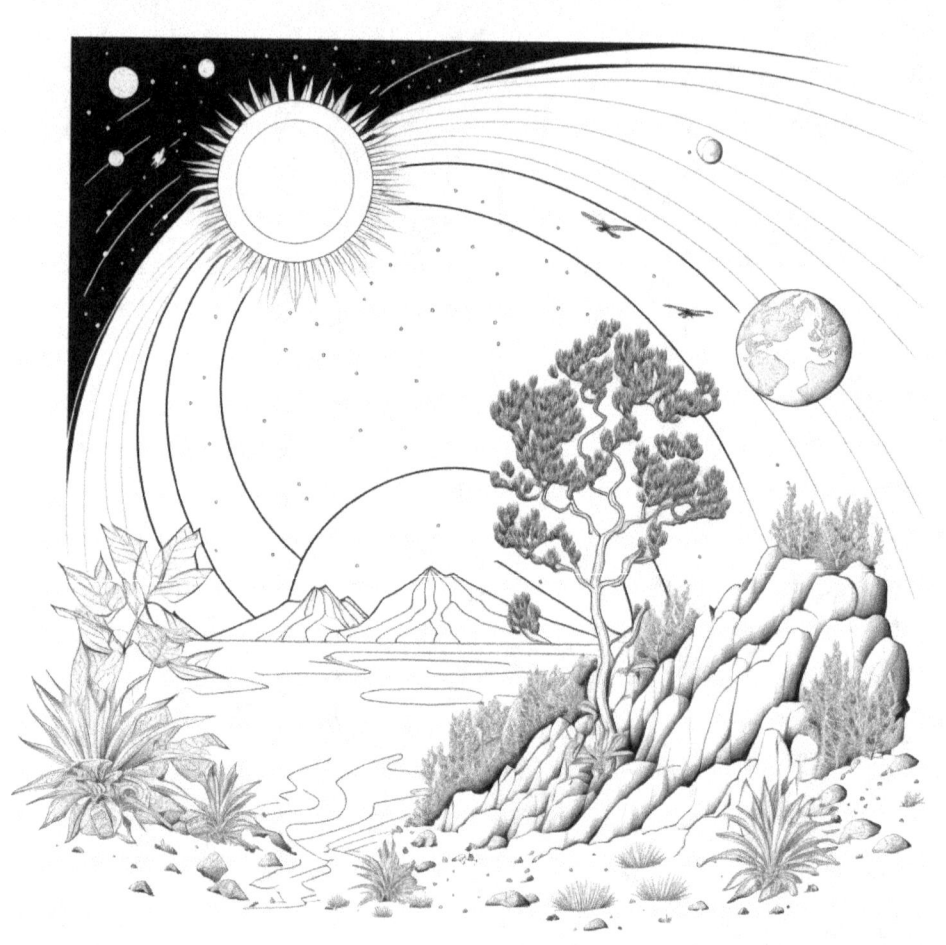

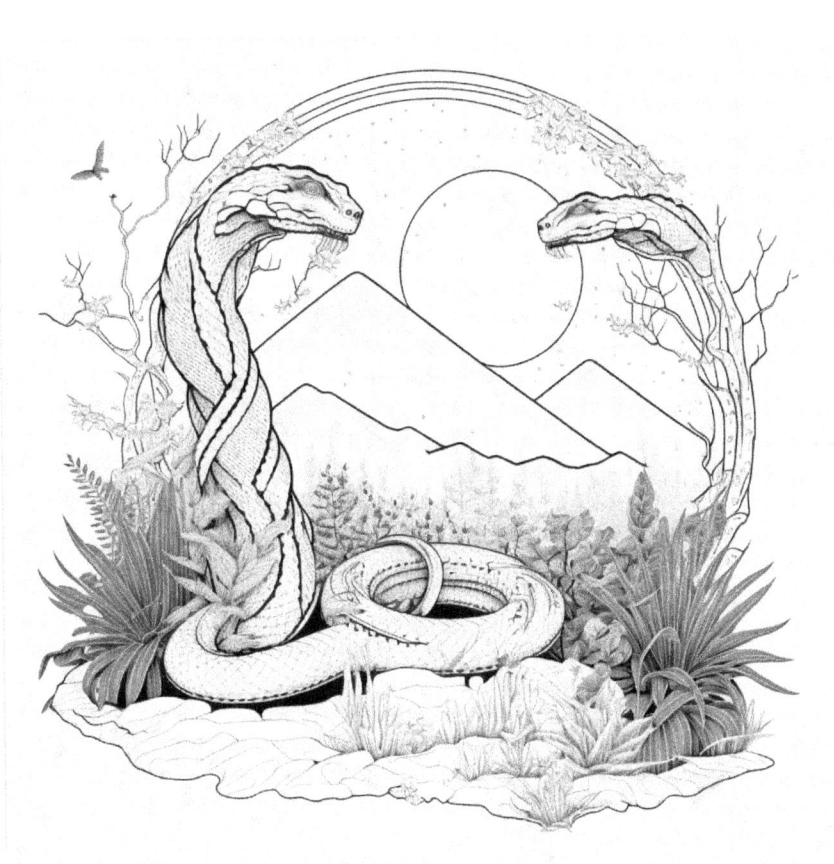

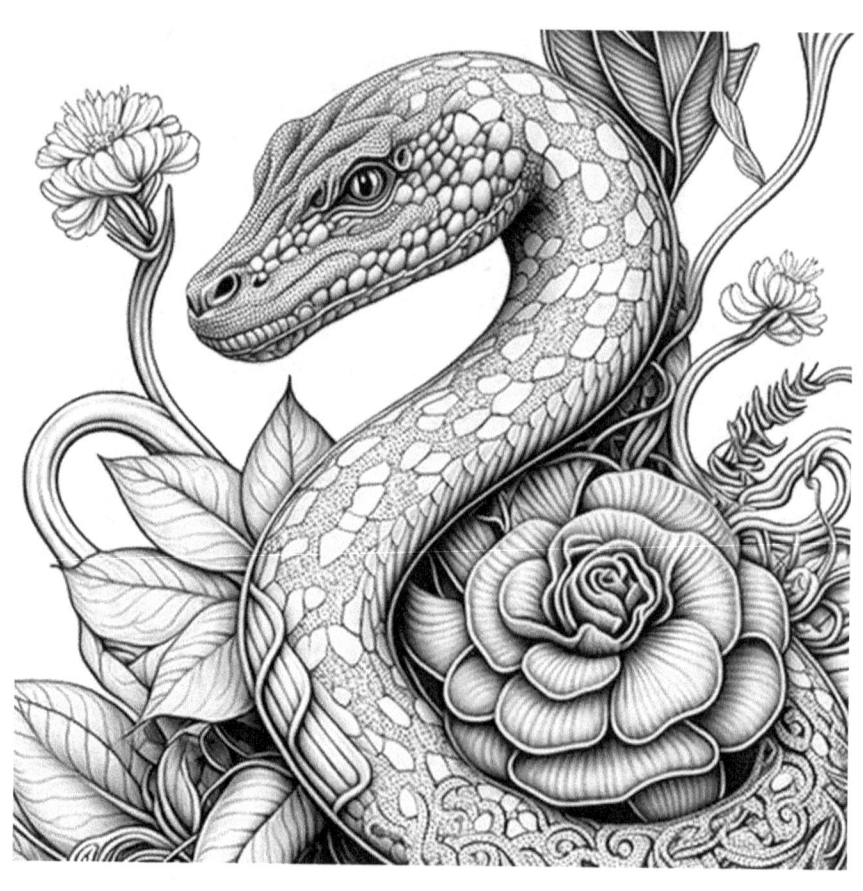

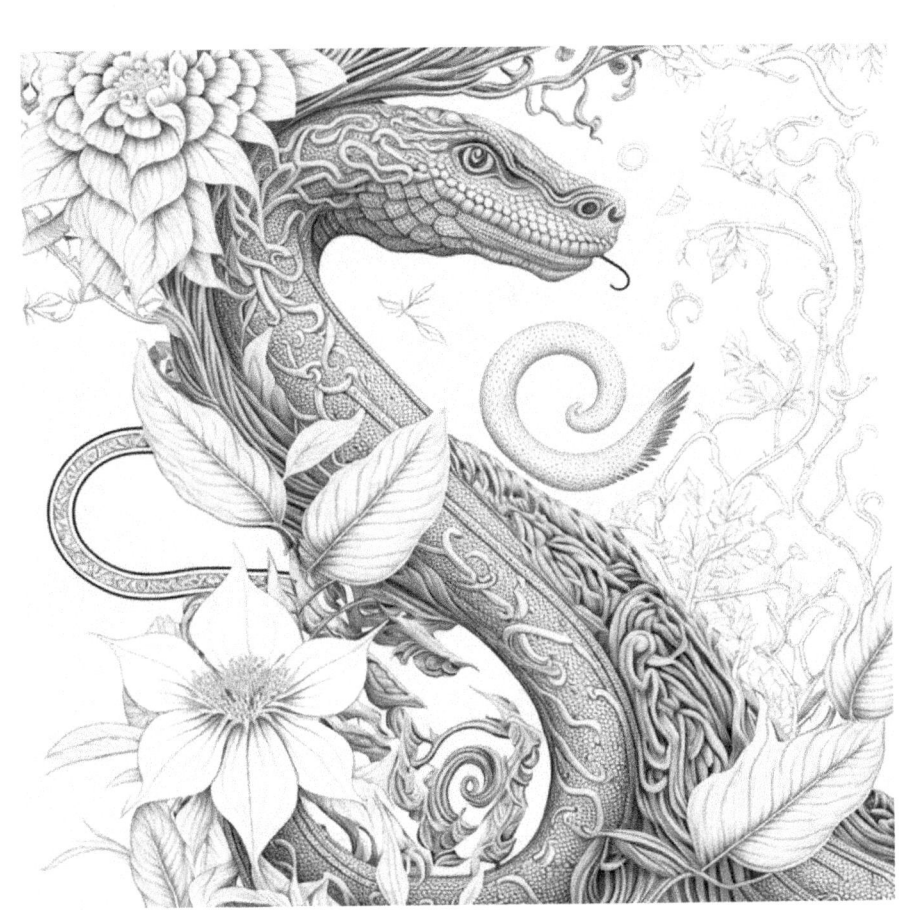

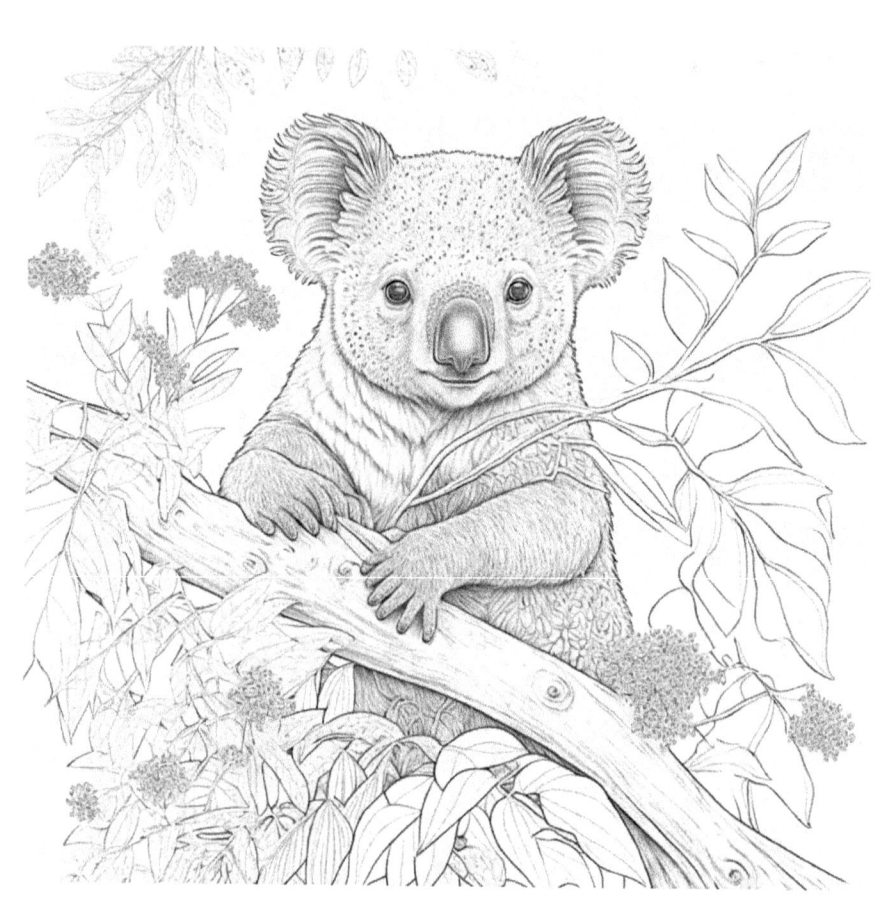

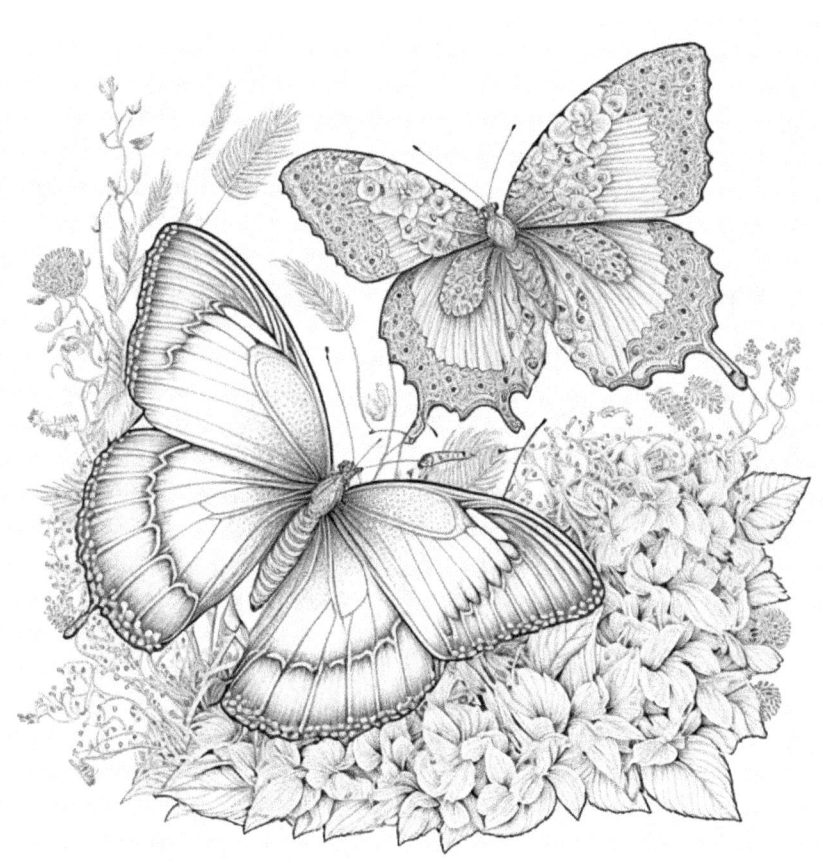

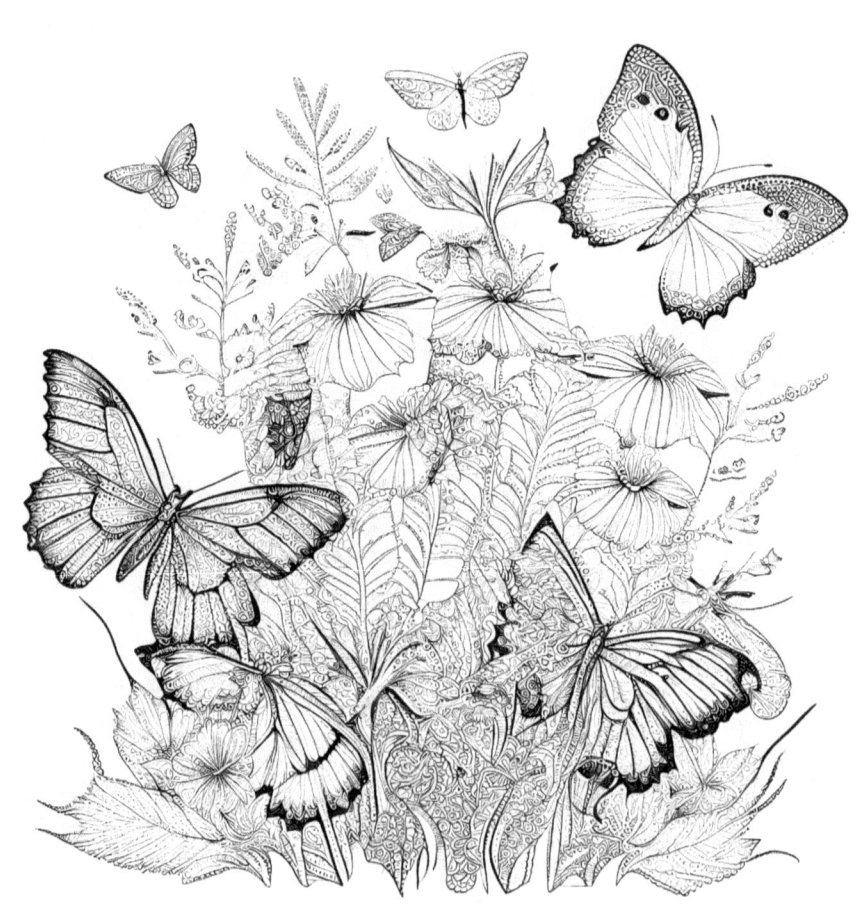

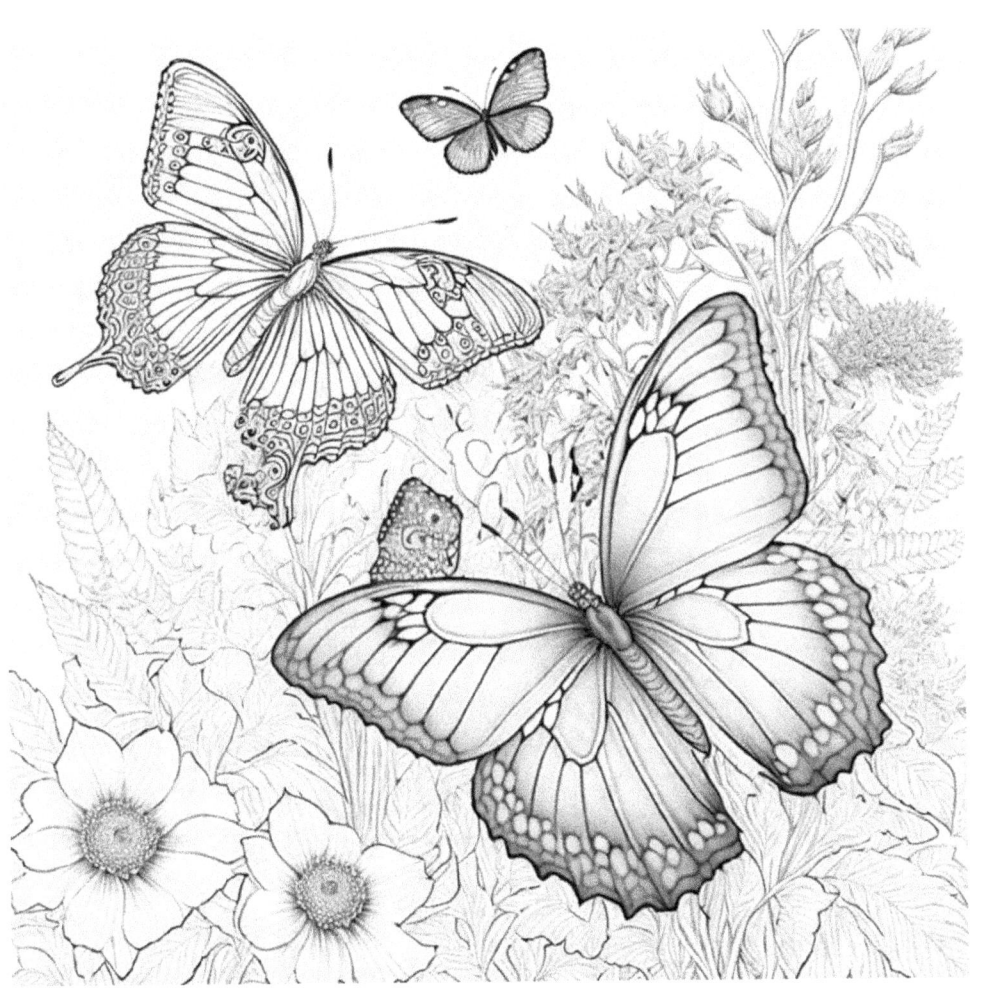

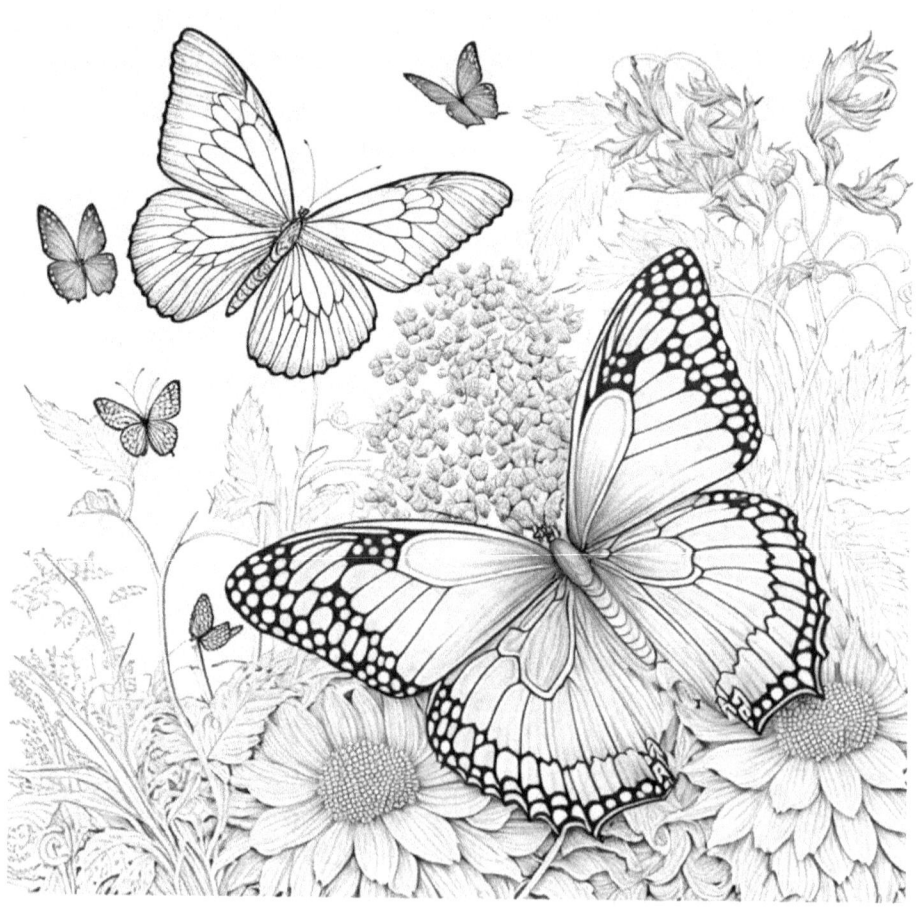

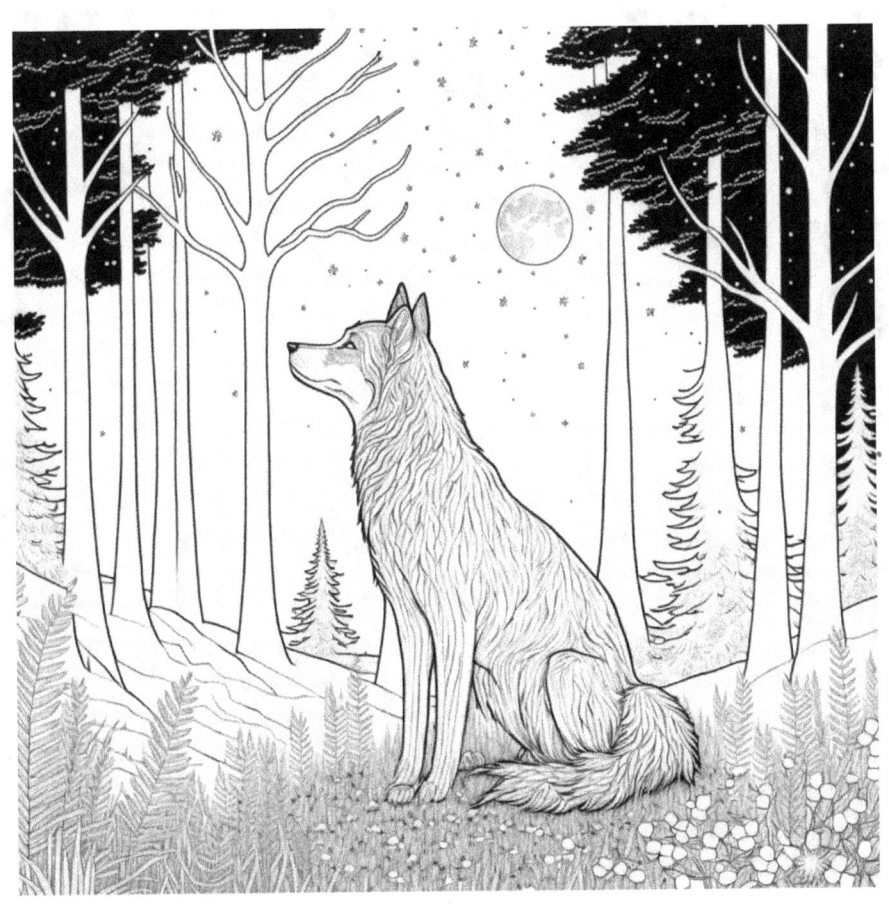

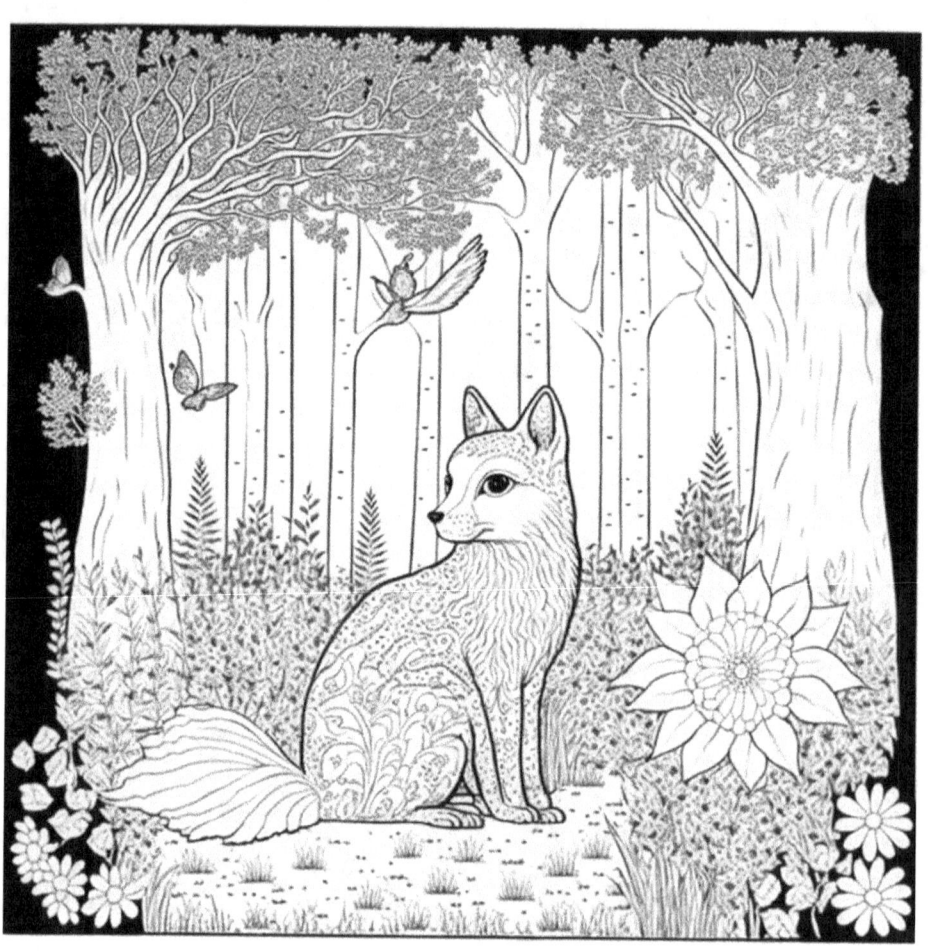

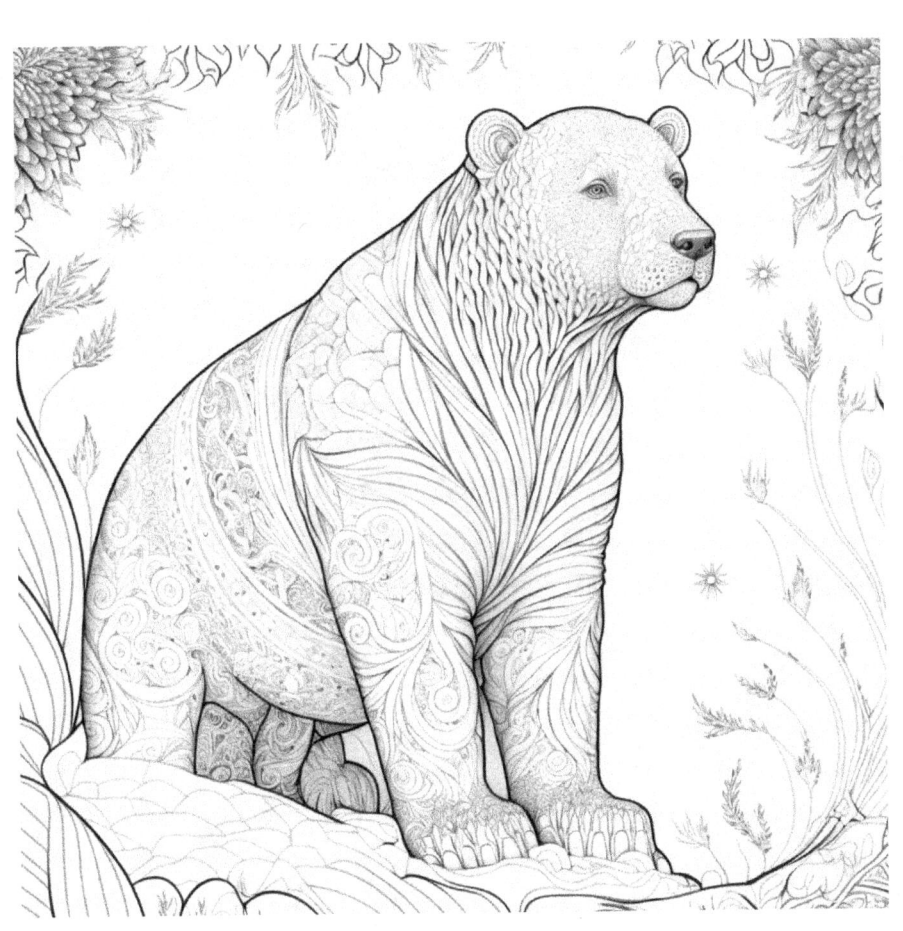

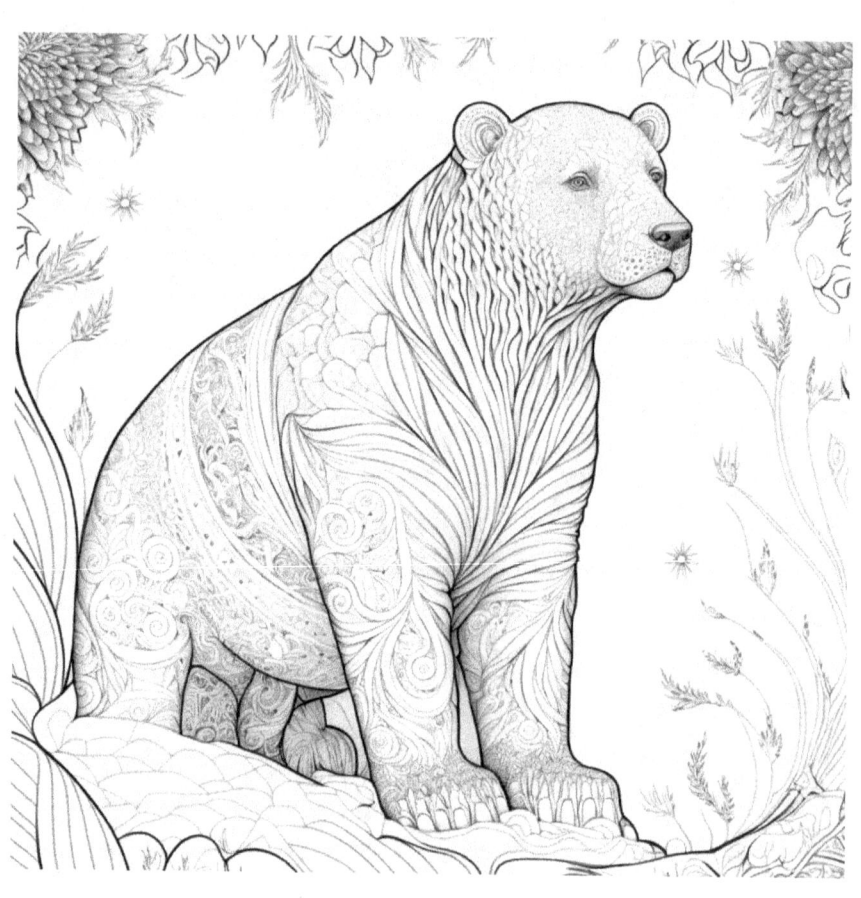

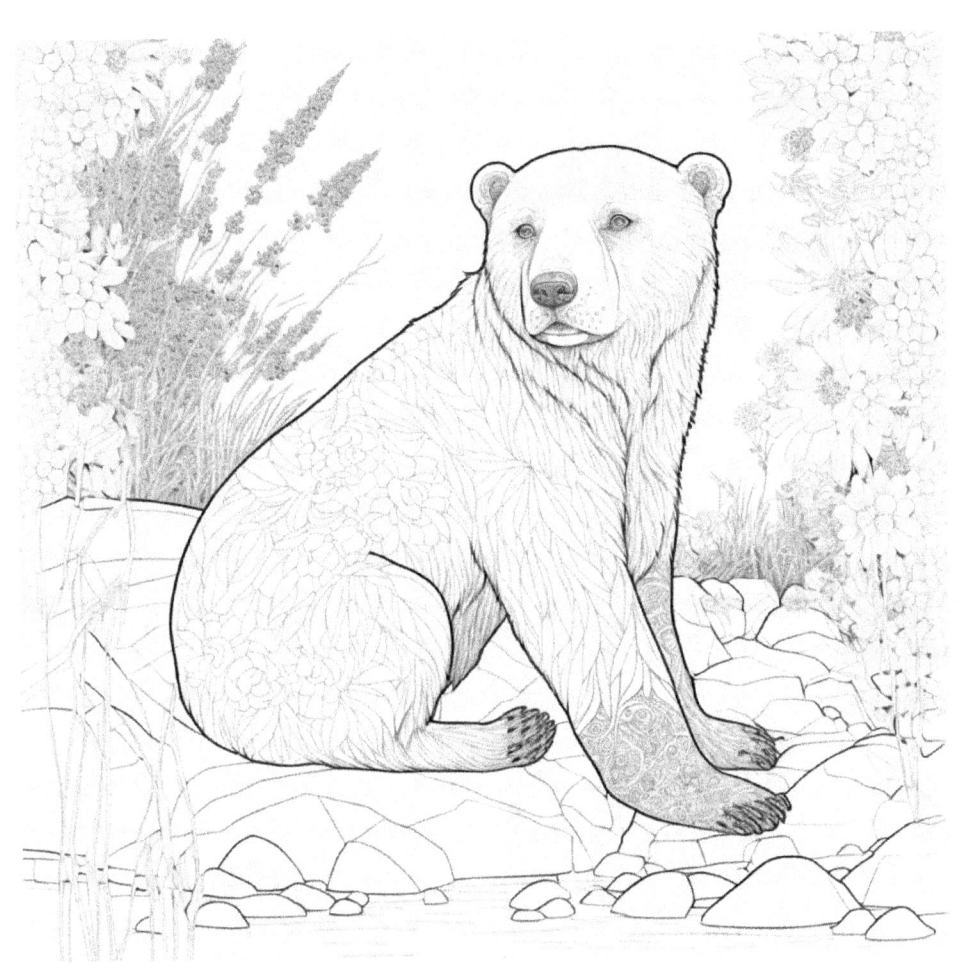

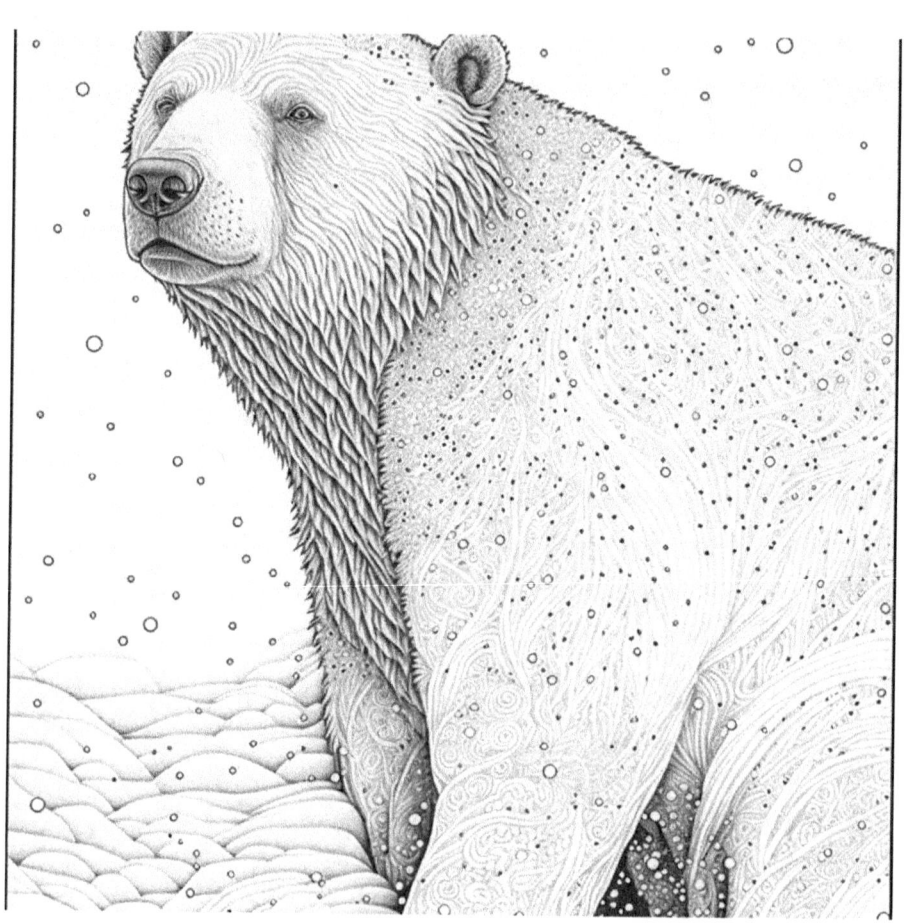

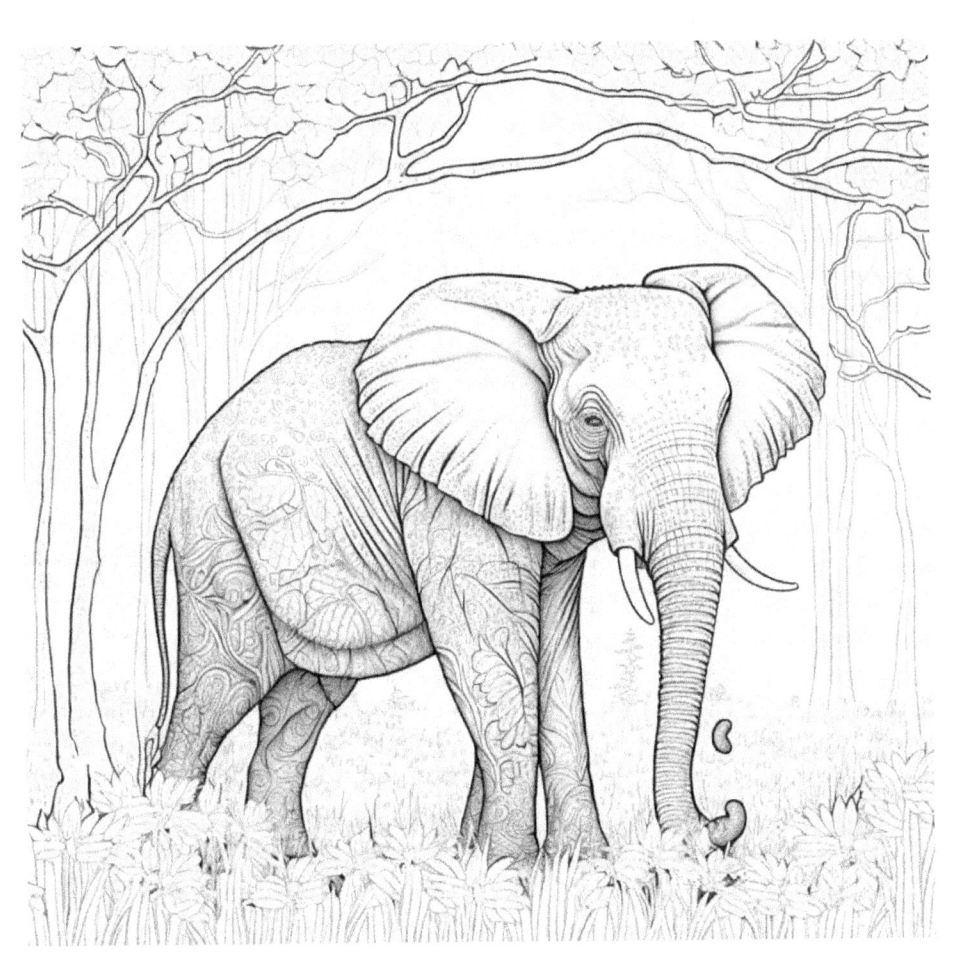

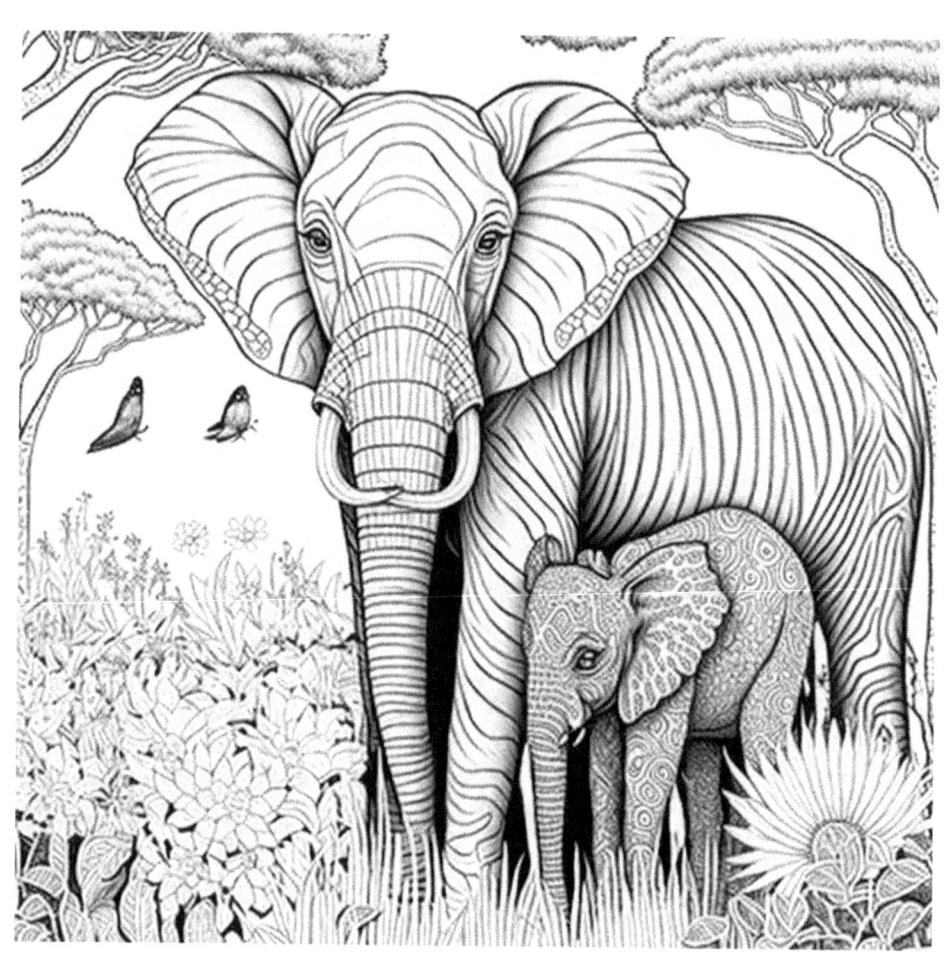

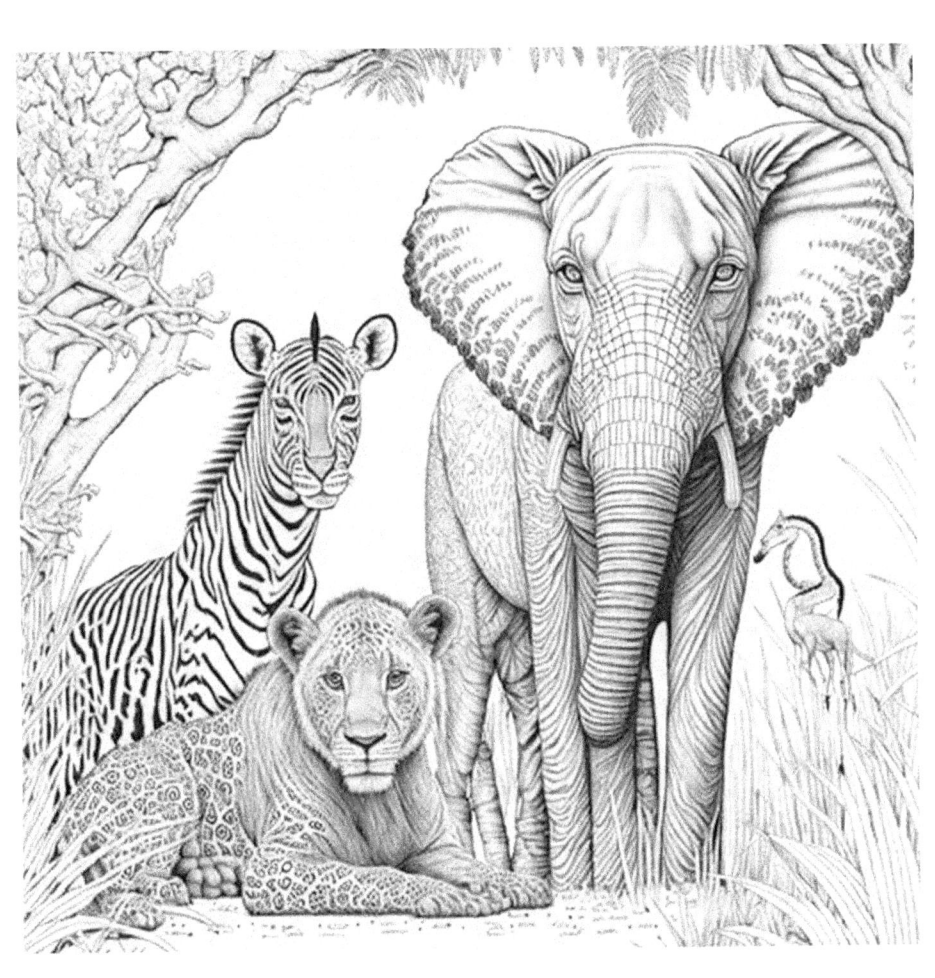

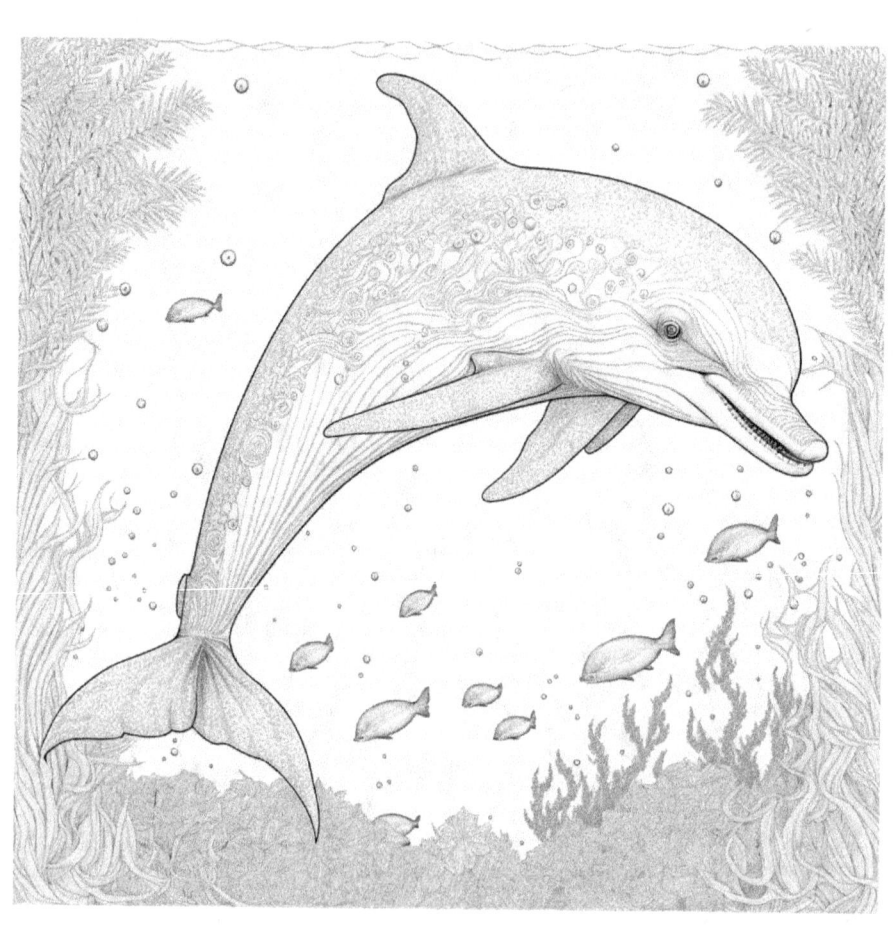

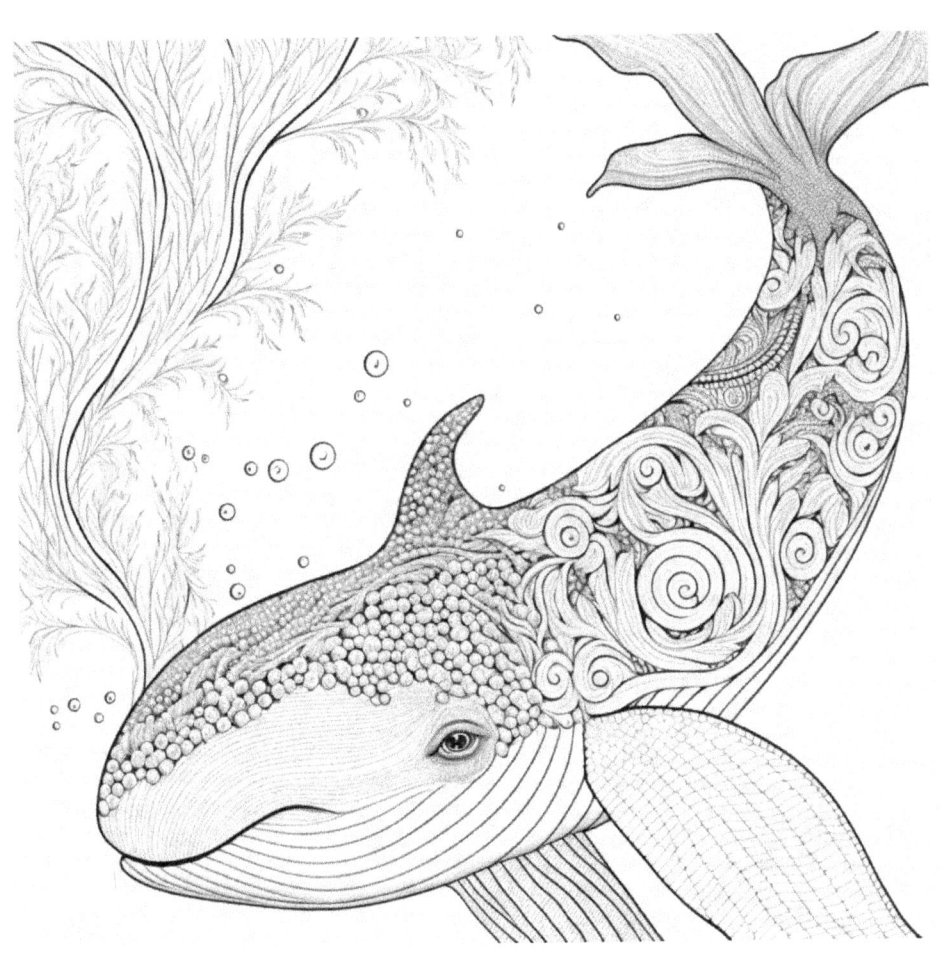

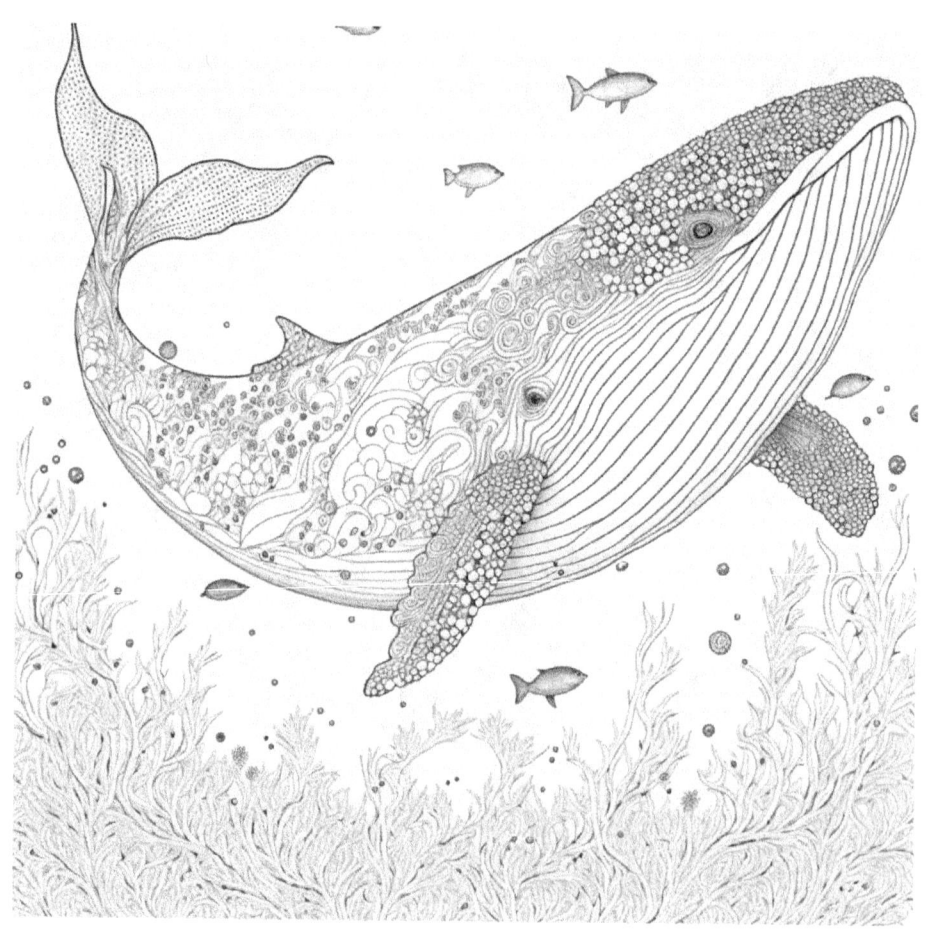

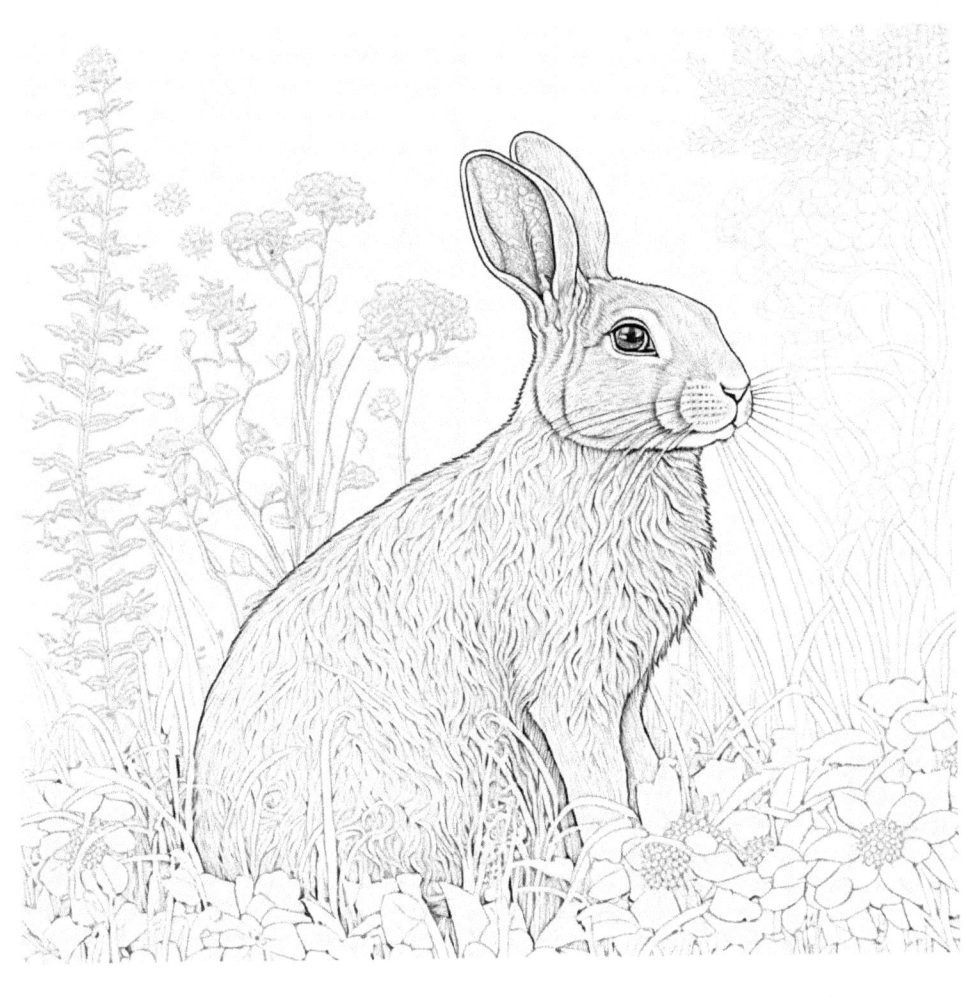

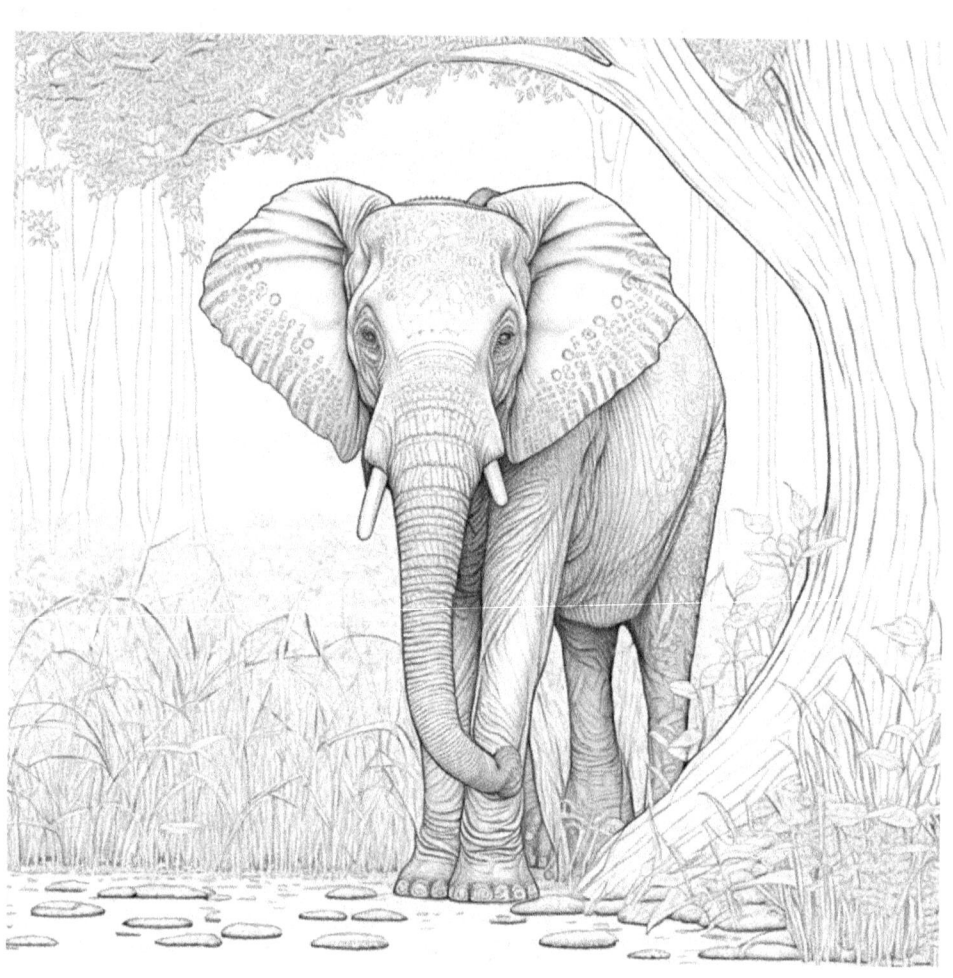

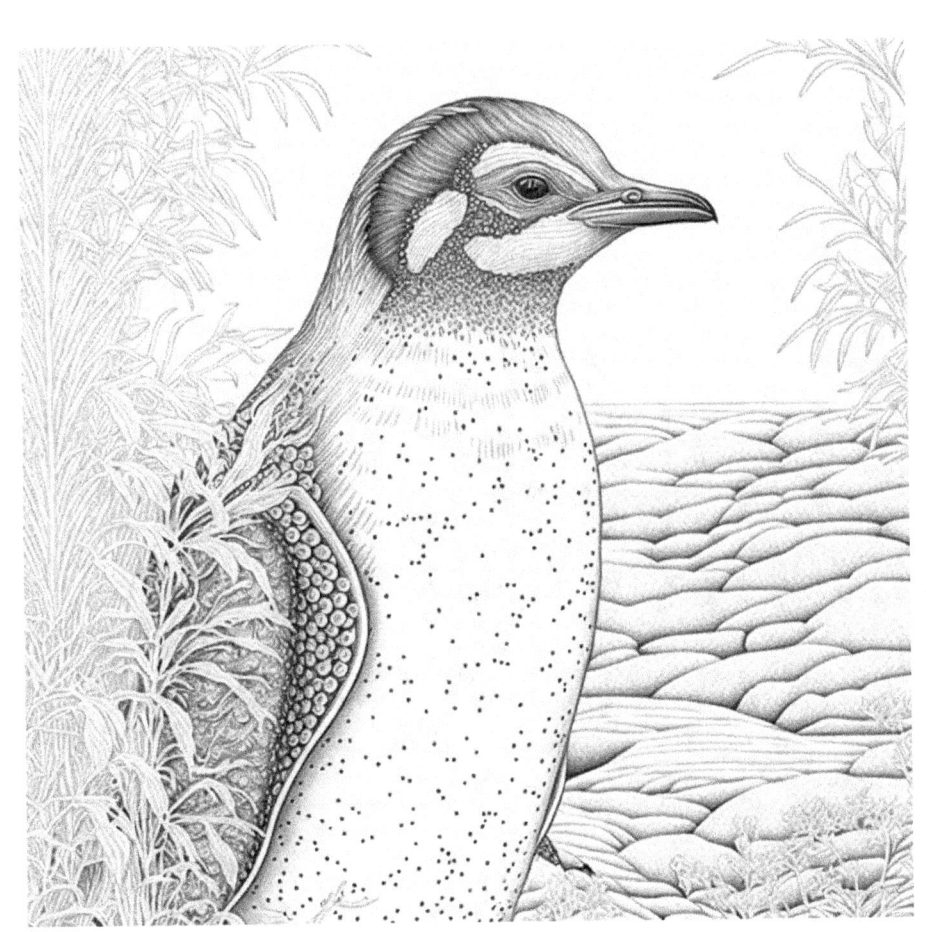

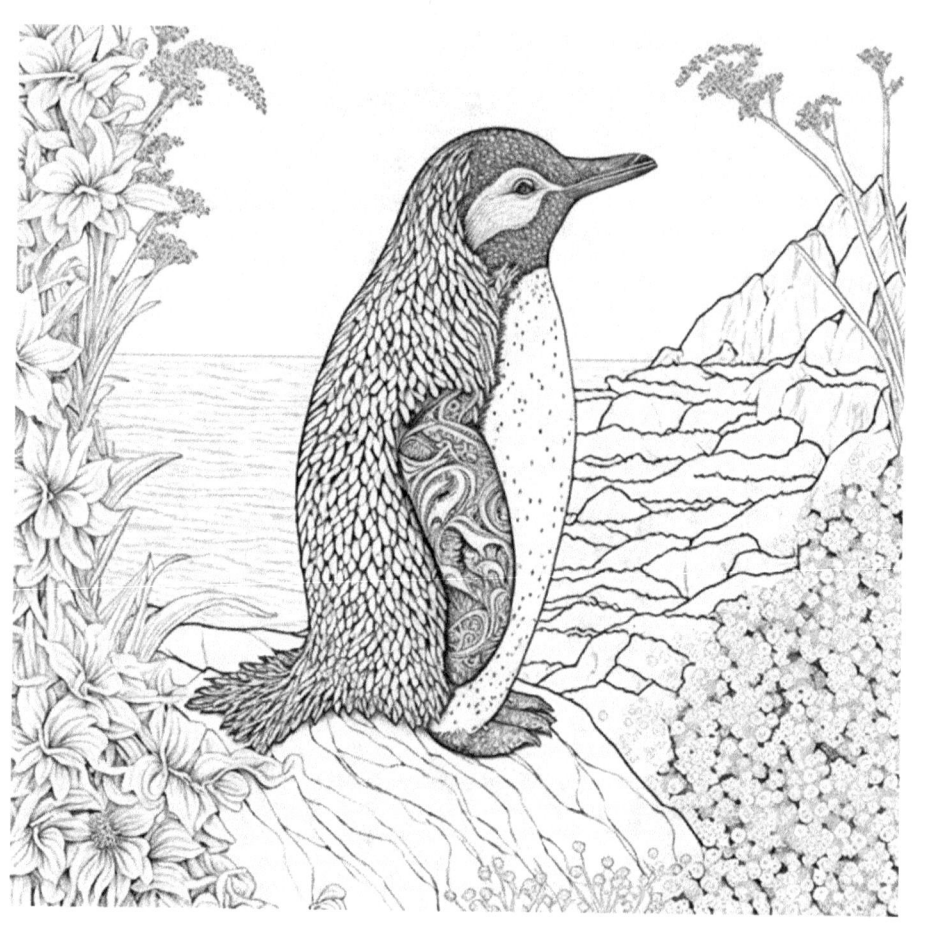

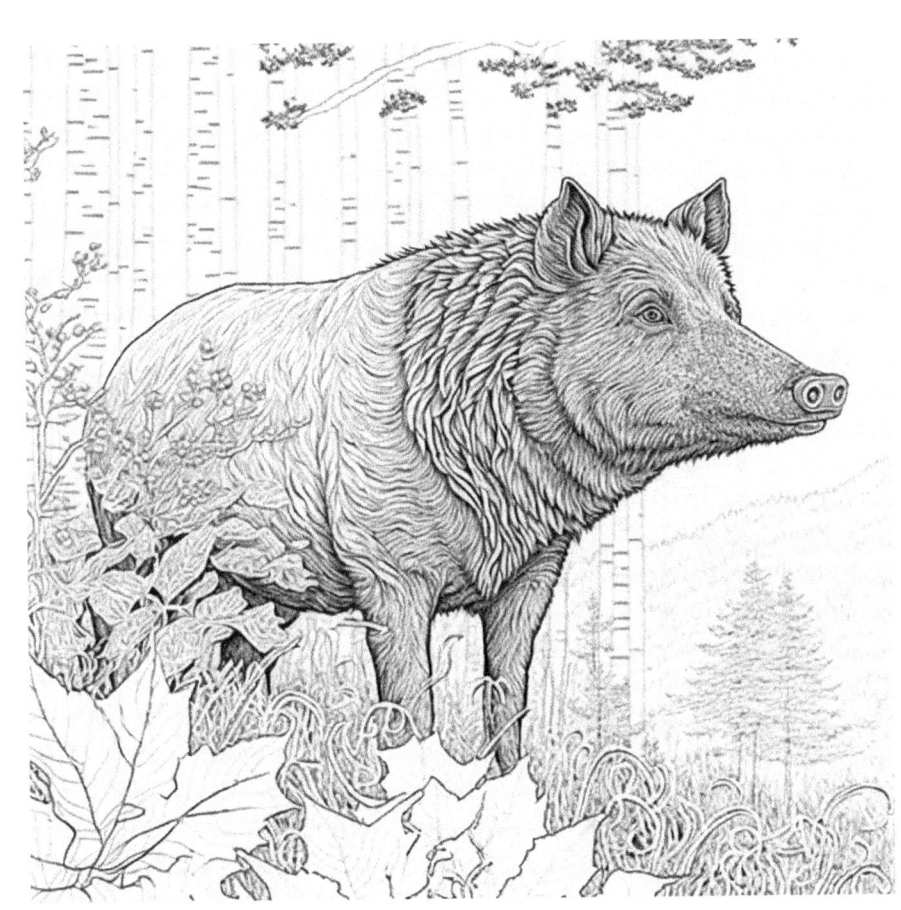

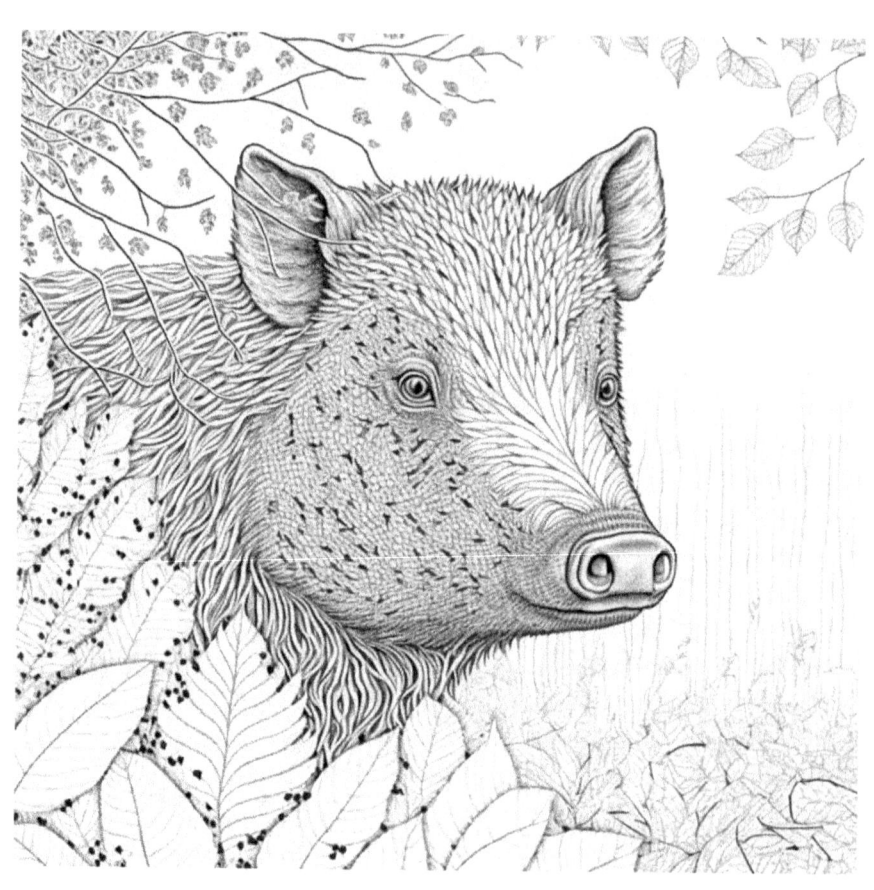

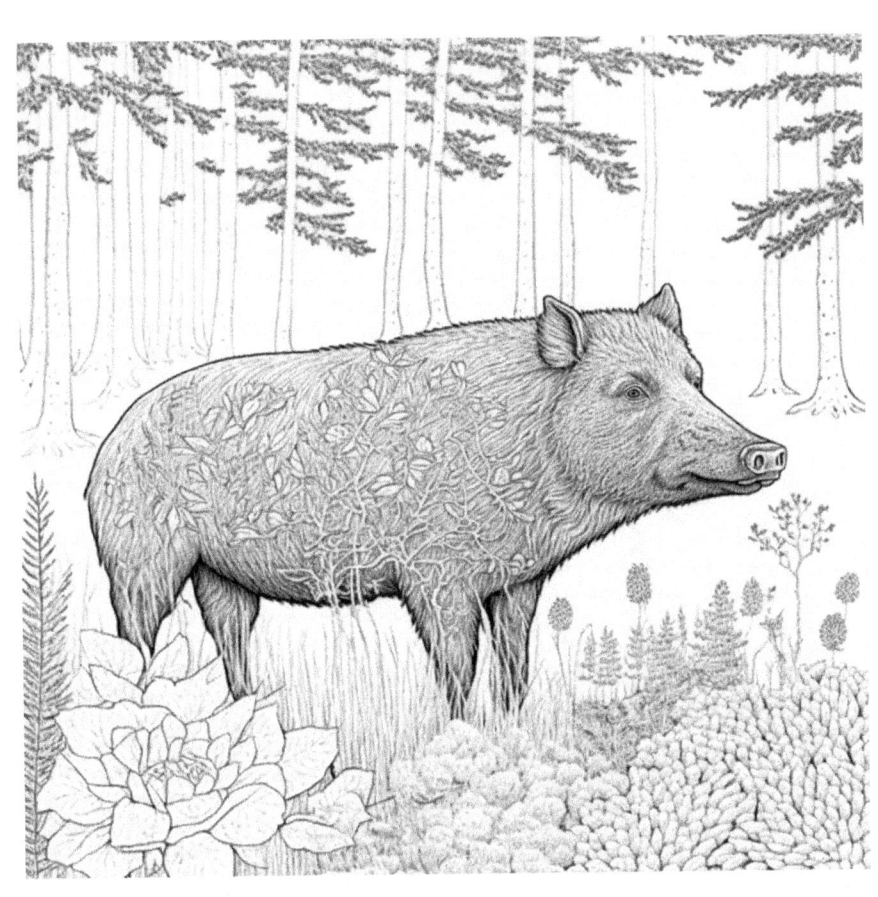

Thank You

www.ingramcontent.com/pod-product-compliance
Lightning Source LLC
Chambersburg PA
CBHW070246220526
45465CB00004B/1541